HOW TO PLAY DUNGEONS AND DRAGONS FOR BEGINNERS

©COPYRIGHT

All rights reserved. No part of this publication may be reproduced, distributed, or transmitted in any form or by any means, including photocopying, recording, or other electronic or mechanical methods, without the prior written permission of the publisher, except in the case of brief quotations embodied in critical reviews and certain other noncommercial uses permitted by copyright law.

☐

TABLE OF CONTENTS

COPYRIGHT   I
TABLE OF CONTENT   II

Chapter 1: Introduction to Dungeons and Dragons

- What is Dungeons and Dragons?
- History and Evolution
- Overview of Editions

Chapter 2: Getting Started   13 - 35

- Basic Rules and Concepts
- Required Materials
- Choosing Your Edition

Chapter 3: Creating Your Character   36

- Understanding Character Sheets
- Races and Classes
- Backgrounds and Alignments
- Abilities and Skills

Chapter 4: Understanding the Game Mechanics

- Dice and Their Uses
- Turn Order and Combat
- Magic and Spellcasting
- Experience and Leveling Up

Chapter 5: Playing the Game   76

- Roleplaying Basics
- Interactions and Social Encounters
- Exploration and Quests
- Combat Strategies

Chapter 6: Dungeon Mastering   95

- Role of the Dungeon Master
- Preparing Your Campaign
- Creating NPCs and Monsters
- Running Encounters and Adventures

Chapter 7: Building Your World   114

- Map Creation and Worldbuilding
- Lore and Storytelling
- Designing Dungeons and Cities
- Crafting Side Quests

Chapter 8: Advanced Gameplay   135 - 149

- Multiclassing and Feats
- Homebrewing Rules and Content
- Complex Combat Tactics
- High-Level Play

Dungeons and Dragons Basics

What is Dungeons and Dragons?

Dungeons and Dragons (D&D) is a tabletop role-playing game (RPG) that has captivated the imaginations of players around the world for nearly five decades. At its core, D&D is a collaborative storytelling game where players create characters who embark on adventures in a fantasy world. The game is guided by a Dungeon Master (DM), who serves as the storyteller and referee, setting the stage for the players' journey, narrating events, and controlling non-player characters (NPCs) and monsters.

Key Elements of Dungeons and Dragons

1. **Role-Playing**: Players assume the roles of their characters, making decisions and taking actions as their characters would. This involves both tactical decisions (such as how to fight a monster) and narrative choices (such as how to negotiate with a king).
2. **Dice-Based Mechanics**: D&D uses a variety of polyhedral dice to determine the outcomes of actions and events. The most common is the 20-sided die (d20), which is used for most attack rolls, skill checks, and saving throws.
3. **Character Creation**: Each player creates a character with a unique combination of race, class, background, and abilities. This

character grows and develops over time, gaining new skills, spells, and equipment as they gain experience.
4. **Storytelling**: The DM weaves together a narrative that responds to the players' actions. The story can be as structured or as open-ended as the DM and players prefer, often including elements like exploration, combat, puzzle-solving, and social interaction.

Example Scenario

Imagine a group of adventurers - a human fighter, an elven wizard, a dwarf cleric, and a halfling rogue - setting out to investigate a series of mysterious disappearances in a small village. As they explore the surrounding forest, they might encounter various challenges: negotiating with a suspicious ranger, solving a puzzle to unlock an ancient ruin, and battling a pack of wolves. Each decision they make and each roll of the dice influences the story, creating a unique and dynamic experience every session.

History and Evolution

Early Beginnings

Dungeons and Dragons was first published in 1974 by Gary Gygax and Dave Arneson. The game originated from tabletop wargaming, where players controlled armies on a battlefield. Gygax and Arneson introduced the concept of individual characters and role-playing, blending elements of storytelling with the tactical depth of wargames. The first edition of D&D was a set of three small booklets, outlining the basic rules for gameplay.

Advanced Dungeons and Dragons (AD&D)

In 1977, TSR (Tactical Studies Rules), the company co-founded by Gygax, released Advanced Dungeons and Dragons (AD&D). This edition expanded and refined the original rules, introducing a more complex and detailed system. AD&D included three core rulebooks: the Player's Handbook, the Dungeon Master's Guide, and the Monster Manual. These books provided comprehensive guidelines for character creation, game mechanics, and world-building, setting the standard for future editions.

The Rise of Popularity and Controversy

Throughout the late 1970s and 1980s, D&D grew in popularity, becoming a cultural phenomenon. It inspired a range of related products, including novels, video games, and a Saturday morning cartoon. However, the game also faced controversy, particularly from religious and parent groups who believed it promoted occultism and satanism.

Despite these challenges, D&D continued to thrive, becoming a beloved pastime for millions of players.

The 2nd Edition and the 1990s

In 1989, TSR released the 2nd Edition of AD&D, which further refined the rules and eliminated some of the more controversial elements. The 2nd Edition emphasized storytelling and character development, introducing new character classes, kits, and a broader range of settings. The game continued to expand its reach, with numerous campaign settings like Forgotten Realms, Dragonlance, and Planescape capturing the imaginations of players.

The Turn of the Millennium: 3rd Edition and 3.5

In 2000, Wizards of the Coast, which had acquired TSR in 1997, released the 3rd Edition of D&D. This edition was a significant overhaul of the rules, introducing the d20 System, which standardized the mechanics for a wide range of actions. The 3rd Edition streamlined gameplay, making it more accessible while maintaining depth and complexity. In 2003, the 3.5 Edition was released, incorporating feedback from players and further refining the rules.

The Controversial 4th Edition

The 4th Edition, released in 2008, marked a significant departure from previous editions. It introduced a more tactical, grid-based combat system and balanced gameplay to ensure that all character classes were equally viable. While some players appreciated the clarity and balance of the 4th Edition, others felt it strayed too far from the storytelling and role-playing elements that defined D&D. This edition sparked significant debate within the D&D community.

The Modern Era: 5th Edition

In 2014, Wizards of the Coast released the 5th Edition of Dungeons and Dragons, which has become the most popular and widely played edition to date. The 5th Edition combines the best elements of previous editions, offering a flexible and accessible system that emphasizes storytelling, character development, and player creativity. It has been praised for its balance between simplicity and depth, making it appealing to both new and experienced players.

The Digital Age and Beyond

In recent years, D&D has experienced a resurgence in popularity, driven by online streaming, podcasts, and digital tools. Shows like "Critical Role" and "Stranger Things" have introduced a new generation to the game, while platforms like Roll20 and D&D Beyond have made it easier to play remotely. The D&D community continues to grow, with players around the world coming together to share their love of the game.

Overview of Editions

Original Dungeons and Dragons (1974)

The original edition of D&D was a groundbreaking game that laid the foundation for all future editions. It consisted of three small booklets: "Men & Magic," "Monsters & Treasure," and "The Underworld & Wilderness Adventures." These booklets provided the basic rules for character creation, combat, and adventure, introducing players to the concept of role-playing games.

Advanced Dungeons and Dragons (1977-1989)

AD&D expanded and refined the original rules, introducing a more complex and detailed system. The core rulebooks included the Player's Handbook, the Dungeon Master's Guide, and the Monster Manual. This edition emphasized tactical gameplay and provided extensive guidelines for creating detailed and immersive campaigns.

2nd Edition (1989)

The 2nd Edition of AD&D continued to refine the rules, eliminating some of the more controversial elements and emphasizing storytelling and character development. New character classes and kits were introduced, along with a broader range of campaign settings. The 2nd Edition also saw the introduction of non-weapon proficiencies, providing more options for character customization.

3rd Edition and 3.5 (2000-2003)

The 3rd Edition marked a significant overhaul of the rules, introducing the d20 System, which standardized the mechanics for a wide range of actions. The 3rd Edition streamlined gameplay, making it more accessible while maintaining depth and complexity. The 3.5 Edition incorporated feedback from players and further refined the rules, improving balance and clarity.

4th Edition (2008)

The 4th Edition introduced a more tactical, grid-based combat system and balanced gameplay to ensure that all character classes were equally viable. This edition emphasized clarity and balance, providing detailed guidelines for creating encounters and adventures. While some players appreciated these changes, others felt it strayed too far from the storytelling and role-playing elements that defined D&D.

5th Edition (2014)

The 5th Edition combines the best elements of previous editions, offering a flexible and accessible system that emphasizes storytelling, character development, and player creativity. It has been praised for its balance between simplicity and depth, making it appealing to both new and experienced players. The 5th Edition has also embraced digital tools and online play, making it easier than ever to connect with other players and share adventures.

In-Depth Example: Creating a Character in 5th Edition

Creating a character in the 5th Edition of D&D involves several steps, each of which allows players to shape their character's identity and abilities. Let's walk through the process with an example character: Elara, a half-elf wizard.

Step 1: Choose a Race

Elara is a half-elf, a race known for their charisma and versatility. Half-elves receive bonuses to their Charisma score and can choose two other ability scores to increase. They also gain proficiency in two skills of their choice and have the ability to see in darkness (darkvision).

Step 2: Choose a Class

Elara is a wizard, a class that specializes in casting spells. Wizards have a high Intelligence score, which determines their spellcasting ability. At 1st level, Elara has a spellbook containing a number of spells and can prepare a certain number of them each day. She also has the Arcane Recovery ability, allowing her to regain some spell slots after a short rest.

Step 3: Determine Ability Scores

Elara's ability scores are determined using one of several methods, such as rolling dice, using a point-buy system, or taking a standard array. Her scores are as follows:

- Strength: 8
- Dexterity: 14
- Constitution: 13
- Intelligence: 16
- Wisdom: 12
- Charisma: 15

These scores reflect her physical and mental capabilities, with Intelligence being her highest score due to her focus on spellcasting.

Step 4: Choose a Background

Elara's background is Sage, reflecting her scholarly pursuits and extensive knowledge. This background grants her proficiency in Arcana and History, two skills related to her studies. It also provides her with additional languages and access to a unique background feature: Researcher, which allows her to find information and resources related to her studies more easily.

Step 5: Select Equipment

Elara starts with basic equipment, including a spellbook, a component pouch for spellcasting materials, and a few simple weapons and tools. As a wizard, she is also proficient with certain types of light armor and weapons, though she relies primarily on her spells in combat.

Step 6: Choose Spells

Elara selects a number of spells from the wizard spell list to add to her spellbook. At 1st level, she has a limited number of spell slots, allowing her to cast a few spells before needing to rest. She chooses spells like Magic Missile, Shield, and Mage Armor, which provide a balance of offensive and defensive capabilities.

Step 7: Flesh Out the Character

Finally, Elara's player adds details to flesh out her character's personality, appearance, and backstory. Elara is described as having a keen intellect and a curious nature, always eager to learn new things and uncover hidden knowledge. She has a mysterious past, having been raised in a secluded elven library, and is driven by a desire to uncover ancient secrets and lost magic.

Through this comprehensive process, players can create unique and engaging characters that fit seamlessly into the world of Dungeons and Dragons. Whether you're new to the game or a seasoned veteran, the joy of D&D lies in the endless possibilities for adventure and creativity.

Getting Started

Basic Rules and Concepts

Introduction

Getting started with Dungeons and Dragons (D&D) involves understanding the fundamental rules and concepts that govern gameplay. This chapter will provide a detailed breakdown of these core elements, including the essential materials you'll need, the structure of the game, and a comprehensive look at the d20 system, which is central to D&D mechanics.

The Core Rulebooks

To play D&D, you typically need access to three core rulebooks:

1. **Player's Handbook (PHB)**: This book contains the rules for character creation, gameplay, combat, equipment, spells, and more. It's essential for players as it guides

them through building and playing their characters.
2. **Dungeon Master's Guide (DMG)**: This book is primarily for the Dungeon Master (DM), providing guidelines for creating and running campaigns, designing adventures, and managing the game.
3. **Monster Manual (MM)**: This book contains detailed descriptions and statistics for various creatures that players might encounter, providing the DM with a rich array of adversaries to challenge the adventurers.

Required Materials

In addition to the core rulebooks, you'll need the following materials to play D&D:

1. **Character Sheets**: These are used to record all the details about a player's character, including their abilities, skills, equipment, and progress.
2. **Dice**: D&D uses a set of polyhedral dice, typically including a d4, d6, d8, d10, d12, and d20. The 20-sided die (d20) is the most commonly used.
3. **Miniatures and Battle Maps**: While not strictly necessary, many players use miniatures and maps to represent characters and visualize combat scenarios.

4. **Pencils and Paper**: Essential for keeping notes, tracking changes to character sheets, and drawing maps.
5. **A Group of Players**: A typical D&D group consists of one DM and several players (usually between 3 to 6).

Understanding the d20 System

The d20 system is the core mechanic used in D&D to resolve actions and determine the outcomes of various events in the game. This system revolves around rolling a 20-sided die (d20) and adding relevant modifiers to determine success or failure.

Key Components of the d20 System

1. **Ability Scores**: Each character has six ability scores that represent their physical and mental attributes: Strength, Dexterity, Constitution, Intelligence, Wisdom, and Charisma. These scores range from 3 to 18 (for most characters) and influence various aspects of gameplay.
2. **Modifiers**: Each ability score has a corresponding modifier, calculated as (ability score - 10) / 2, rounded down. These modifiers are added to dice rolls to determine outcomes.
3. **Proficiency Bonus**: Characters have a proficiency bonus that increases as they level

up. This bonus is added to rolls for skills, attacks, and saving throws in which the character is proficient.
4. **Skill Checks**: To perform a task that has an uncertain outcome (e.g., picking a lock, deciphering a script), a player makes a skill check by rolling a d20 and adding the relevant ability modifier and proficiency bonus if applicable.
5. **Saving Throws**: These rolls are made to resist harmful effects, such as poisons or spells. Like skill checks, they involve rolling a d20 and adding the relevant ability modifier and proficiency bonus.
6. **Attack Rolls**: When a character attacks, they roll a d20 and add their attack bonus (which includes their ability modifier and proficiency bonus if they are proficient with the weapon). The result is compared to the target's Armor Class (AC) to determine if the attack hits.
7. **Difficulty Class (DC)**: The DM sets a DC for tasks and challenges. The result of a d20 roll plus relevant modifiers must meet or exceed the DC to succeed.

Examples of the d20 System in Action

Skill Check Example

Elara, the half-elf wizard, wants to decipher an ancient text. The DM decides this requires an Intelligence (Arcana) check. Elara has an Intelligence modifier of +3 and proficiency in Arcana (+2 proficiency bonus).

- Elara's player rolls a d20 and gets a 14.
- The total roll is 14 (d20) + 3 (Intelligence modifier) + 2 (proficiency bonus) = 19.
- The DM has set the DC at 15. Elara succeeds in deciphering the text.

Saving Throw Example

Elara is targeted by a fireball spell and needs to make a Dexterity saving throw to avoid taking full damage. She has a Dexterity modifier of +2 but no proficiency in Dexterity saving throws.

- Elara's player rolls a d20 and gets a 10.
- The total roll is 10 (d20) + 2 (Dexterity modifier) = 12.
- The DC for the fireball spell is 14. Elara fails the saving throw and takes full damage.

Attack Roll Example

Elara's companion, a human fighter named Garrick, swings his sword at an orc. Garrick has a Strength modifier of +3 and is proficient with his sword (+2 proficiency bonus).

- Garrick's player rolls a d20 and gets a 15.
- The total roll is 15 (d20) + 3 (Strength modifier) + 2 (proficiency bonus) = 20.
- The orc has an AC of 16. Garrick's attack hits, and he rolls for damage.

Turn Structure and Actions

D&D gameplay is typically divided into turns, especially during combat. Each turn consists of the following components:

1. **Initiative**: At the start of combat, all participants roll for initiative, which determines the order in which they take their turns. Initiative is a d20 roll plus the character's Dexterity modifier.
2. **Actions**: On their turn, a character can perform one action. Actions include attacking, casting a spell, dashing, disengaging, dodging, and more.
3. **Bonus Actions**: Certain abilities and spells allow characters to take an additional bonus action on their turn.
4. **Movement**: Characters can move up to their speed (in feet) on their turn. Movement can be split before and after actions.
5. **Reactions**: Characters can take one reaction outside of their turn in response to a specific trigger, such as an enemy moving out of their reach (opportunity attack).

Example Turn Sequence

In a combat scenario, Elara, Garrick, and their allies face off against a group of goblins. Here's how a turn might play out:

1. **Initiative Roll**:
    - Elara rolls a d20 and adds her Dexterity modifier (+2), getting a total of 15.
    - Garrick rolls a d20 and adds his Dexterity modifier (+1), getting a total of 12.
    - The DM rolls for the goblins, who get a total of 18.

    The initiative order is: Goblins, Elara, Garrick.

2. **Goblin's Turn**:
    - The goblins move towards the party and attack. One goblin swings at Garrick but misses.
3. **Elara's Turn**:
    - Elara decides to cast Magic Missile, an automatic hit spell. She rolls for damage and deals 12 points to one of the goblins.
4. **Garrick's Turn**:
    - Garrick moves into position and attacks a goblin with his sword,

rolling a d20 and adding his attack bonus. He hits and rolls for damage, defeating the goblin.

Using Ability Scores

Ability scores play a crucial role in shaping what characters can do and how effectively they perform various tasks. Here's a closer look at how each ability score impacts gameplay:

1. **Strength**: Measures physical power and carrying capacity. It influences melee attack rolls, damage rolls, and athletic skill checks.
    - Example: Garrick tries to break down a door. The DM asks for a Strength (Athletics) check. Garrick rolls a d20, adds his Strength modifier, and any proficiency bonus.
2. **Dexterity**: Measures agility, reflexes, and balance. It influences ranged attack rolls, AC, and skills like Acrobatics and Stealth.
    - Example: Elara attempts to sneak past a guard. She makes a Dexterity (Stealth) check, rolling a d20 and adding her Dexterity modifier and proficiency bonus.
3. **Constitution**: Measures endurance and stamina. It affects hit points (HP) and saving throws against effects like poison.

- Example: Elara drinks a suspicious potion. The DM asks for a Constitution saving throw to resist any negative effects.
4. **Intelligence**: Measures reasoning and memory. It influences skills like Arcana, History, and Investigation.
    - Example: Elara examines a magical artifact. The DM asks for an Intelligence (Arcana) check to identify its properties.
5. **Wisdom**: Measures perception and insight. It influences skills like Perception, Insight, and Survival.
    - Example: Garrick tries to sense if someone is lying. He makes a Wisdom (Insight) check, rolling a d20 and adding his Wisdom modifier.
6. **Charisma**: Measures force of personality and social influence. It influences skills like Persuasion, Deception, and Intimidation.
    - Example: Elara tries to persuade a merchant to lower their prices. She makes a Charisma (Persuasion) check, rolling a d20 and adding her Charisma modifier and proficiency bonus.

Difficulty Class (DC) and Task Resolution

The DM sets the Difficulty Class (DC) for tasks and challenges based on how hard they are. Here's a general guideline for setting DCs:

- Very Easy (DC 5): Requires little effort.
- Easy (DC 10): Requires a small amount of effort.
- Moderate (DC 15): Requires some effort.
- Hard (DC 20): Requires significant effort.
- Very Hard (DC 25): Requires exceptional effort.
- Nearly Impossible (DC 30): Requires an extraordinary effort.

Example: Task Resolution

Elara wants to climb a steep cliff to get a better view. The DM sets the DC at 15, considering it a moderately challenging task.

- Elara makes a Strength (Athletics) check. She rolls a d20 and adds her Strength modifier (+1) and proficiency bonus if she's proficient in Athletics (+2).
- She rolls a 13 on the d20, so her total is 13 + 1 + 2 = 16. Elara successfully climbs the cliff.

Conclusion

Understanding the basic rules and concepts of D&D is essential for both players and Dungeon Masters.

The d20 system forms the backbone of gameplay, providing a consistent and flexible framework for resolving actions and events. By mastering these fundamentals, you'll be well-equipped to create and explore the rich, immersive worlds that make Dungeons and Dragons an enduring and beloved game.

Required Materials

Core Rulebooks

The core rulebooks are essential for understanding the rules and mechanics of Dungeons and Dragons (D&D). These books provide comprehensive guidelines for both players and Dungeon Masters (DMs), ensuring a smooth and enjoyable gaming experience.

1. **Player's Handbook (PHB)**
    - **Content**: The PHB is the primary reference for players, containing rules for character creation, gameplay mechanics, equipment, spells, and much more. It introduces the basic concepts of D&D, helping players understand their roles in the game.
    - **Importance**: Every player should have access to a PHB, as it contains detailed explanations of races, classes, backgrounds, skills, and feats. It also

provides information on how to level up characters and manage their progression throughout the game.
- **Example**: The PHB explains how to create a character like Elara, a half-elf wizard, by detailing her race, class, abilities, spells, and equipment.

2. **Dungeon Master's Guide (DMG)**
    - **Content**: The DMG is tailored for the Dungeon Master, offering advice on how to run a game, create adventures, design encounters, and manage the game world. It includes optional rules, guidelines for creating NPCs and monsters, and tips for storytelling.
    - **Importance**: The DMG is crucial for DMs as it provides the tools needed to craft engaging and balanced campaigns. It helps DMs navigate the complexities of the game and maintain the flow of the narrative.
    - **Example**: The DMG includes instructions on how to create a compelling campaign setting, complete with maps, lore, and plot hooks that engage players like Elara and her companions.

3. **Monster Manual (MM)**

- **Content**: The MM is a comprehensive collection of creatures that players might encounter during their adventures. It provides detailed descriptions, statistics, and abilities for a wide range of monsters, from common goblins to powerful dragons.
- **Importance**: The MM is essential for DMs to populate their world with diverse and challenging creatures. It helps DMs design encounters that test the skills and strategies of the players.
- **Example**: When Elara and her party venture into a dungeon, the DM can use the MM to find suitable monsters to challenge them, such as a group of goblins guarding a treasure hoard.

Dice

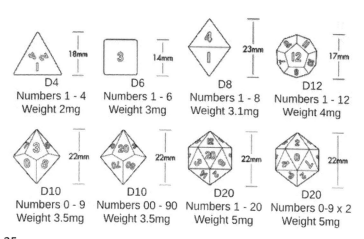

D4
Numbers 1 - 4
Weight 2mg

D6
Numbers 1 - 6
Weight 3mg

D8
Numbers 1 - 8
Weight 3.1mg

D12
Numbers 1 - 12
Weight 4mg

D10
Numbers 0 - 9
Weight 3.5mg

D10
Numbers 00 - 90
Weight 3.5mg

D20
Numbers 1 - 20
Weight 5mg

D20
Numbers 0-9 x 2
Weight 5mg

D&D uses a set of polyhedral dice to determine the outcomes of actions and events. The most commonly used dice include:

1. **d20 (20-sided die)**: Used for most attack rolls, skill checks, and saving throws. The d20 system is the backbone of D&D's mechanics.
2. **d12 (12-sided die)**: Often used for damage rolls, especially for certain weapons or spells.
3. **d10 (10-sided die)**: Used for various damage rolls and percentage checks.
4. **d8 (8-sided die)**: Commonly used for damage rolls and some healing spells.
5. **d6 (6-sided die)**: Used for damage rolls, ability score rolls, and more.
6. **d4 (4-sided die)**: Often used for smaller damage rolls and certain spell effects.

Example: Using Dice in Gameplay

Elara casts a fireball spell, which requires a damage roll of 8d6 (eight 6-sided dice). She rolls a total of 32 damage. Each affected creature makes a Dexterity saving throw (using a d20) to determine if they take full or half damage.

Character Sheets

Character sheets are essential tools for tracking all aspects of a player's character. They include sections for:

1. **Basic Information**: Character name, race, class, background, and alignment.
2. **Ability Scores**: Strength, Dexterity, Constitution, Intelligence, Wisdom, and Charisma, along with their modifiers.
3. **Skills and Proficiencies**: Skills the character is proficient in, along with their corresponding ability modifiers and proficiency bonus.
4. **Equipment**: Weapons, armor, magical items, and other gear.
5. **Spells**: For spellcasters, a list of known spells, spell slots, and spell save DCs.
6. **Hit Points and Conditions**: Current and maximum hit points, temporary hit points, and any conditions affecting the character.

Example: Elara's Character Sheet

Elara's character sheet includes her race (half-elf), class (wizard), ability scores (e.g., Intelligence 16), skills (e.g., Arcana proficiency), equipment (e.g., spellbook, component pouch), and spells (e.g., Magic Missile, Shield).

Miniatures and Battle Maps

While not strictly necessary, miniatures and battle maps enhance the visual and tactical aspects of D&D. They help players visualize combat and movement within the game world.

1. **Miniatures**: Small figures representing characters, monsters, and NPCs. They can be purchased or custom-made.
2. **Battle Maps**: Gridded maps used to represent various locations, such as dungeons, towns, or wilderness areas. They help track movement and positioning during encounters.

Example: Using Miniatures and Maps

During a dungeon crawl, the DM uses a battle map to depict the layout of the dungeon. Elara's player moves her miniature across the map, navigating traps and engaging enemies positioned by the DM.

Pencils and Paper

Pencils and paper are essential for taking notes, tracking changes to character sheets, and drawing maps. They allow players to record important information, such as quest details, loot, and NPC interactions.

A Group of Players

A typical D&D group consists of one DM and several players (usually between 3 to 6). The group dynamic is crucial for a successful game, as players work together to overcome challenges and tell their collective story.

Choosing Your Edition

Dungeons and Dragons has evolved through several editions, each offering unique rules, mechanics, and playstyles. Choosing the right edition for your group depends on your preferences, experience, and desired gameplay experience.

Original Dungeons and Dragons (1974)

The original edition of D&D introduced the concept of tabletop role-playing games. It consisted of three small booklets that provided the basic rules for gameplay. This edition laid the foundation for all future versions of the game.

Characteristics

- **Simple Mechanics**: Basic rules for character creation, combat, and magic.
- **Focused on Exploration**: Emphasis on dungeon crawling and exploration.
- **Limited Options**: Fewer races and classes compared to later editions.

Example: Playing Original D&D

In an original D&D game, Elara might be a human magic-user exploring a dungeon filled with traps and monsters. The focus would be on navigating the dungeon and surviving its perils.

Advanced Dungeons and Dragons (AD&D)

AD&D, released in 1977, expanded and refined the original rules, introducing more complex mechanics and a broader range of options. It included three core rulebooks: the Player's Handbook, the Dungeon Master's Guide, and the Monster Manual.

Characteristics

- **Complex Mechanics**: More detailed rules for character creation, combat, and magic.
- **Expanded Options**: A wider variety of races, classes, spells, and equipment.
- **Emphasis on Tactical Play**: More focus on tactical combat and strategic planning.

Example: Playing AD&D

In an AD&D game, Elara might be a half-elf mage, using a combination of spells and tactics to overcome enemies. The game would involve more detailed character creation and complex combat scenarios.

2nd Edition (1989)

The 2nd Edition of AD&D continued to refine the rules and eliminate some controversial elements. It emphasized storytelling and character development, introducing new character classes, kits, and campaign settings.

Characteristics

- **Refined Mechanics**: Streamlined rules for a smoother gameplay experience.
- **Focus on Storytelling**: Greater emphasis on narrative and character development.
- **Diverse Settings**: Introduction of iconic campaign settings like Forgotten Realms and Dragonlance.

Example: Playing 2nd Edition

In a 2nd Edition game, Elara might be part of a story-driven campaign set in the Forgotten Realms. Her character's background and motivations would play a significant role in the unfolding narrative.

3rd Edition and 3.5 (2000-2003)

The 3rd Edition marked a significant overhaul of the rules, introducing the d20 System, which standardized mechanics across actions. The 3.5 Edition incorporated feedback from players and further refined the rules.

Characteristics

- **d20 System**: A unified mechanic using a 20-sided die for most actions.
- **Flexibility and Customization**: Extensive options for character customization through feats, skills, and multiclassing.
- **Balanced Gameplay**: Improved balance between different character classes.

Example: Playing 3rd Edition

In a 3rd Edition game, Elara could be a highly customized wizard with a unique combination of feats and skills. The game would offer a flexible and balanced system for both combat and role-playing.

4th Edition (2008)

The 4th Edition introduced a more tactical, grid-based combat system and focused on balanced gameplay. It aimed to provide clarity and balance among character classes.

Characteristics

- **Tactical Combat**: Grid-based combat with a focus on positioning and strategy.
- **Clear Roles**: Defined roles for each class (e.g., defender, striker, controller).
- **Balanced Classes**: Efforts to ensure all classes are equally viable and effective.

Example: Playing 4th Edition

In a 4th Edition game, Elara might be a controller wizard, using her spells to manipulate the battlefield and support her allies. The game would involve detailed combat encounters with an emphasis on tactics.

5th Edition (2014)

The 5th Edition of D&D aimed to combine the best elements of previous editions, offering streamlined rules, flexibility, and a focus on storytelling. It is currently the most popular and widely played edition.

Characteristics

- **Streamlined Mechanics**: Simplified rules for ease of play and accessibility.
- **Focus on Role-Playing**: Emphasis on storytelling, character development, and narrative.

- **Flexibility and Options**: A wide range of character options, including backgrounds, subclasses, and feats.

Example: Playing 5th Edition

In a 5th Edition game, Elara might be a half-elf wizard with a rich backstory and a unique combination of spells and abilities. The game would focus on both role-playing and tactical combat, offering a balanced and immersive experience.

Choosing the Right Edition

When choosing an edition, consider the following factors:

1. **Player Preferences**: What do your players enjoy most about D&D? Do they prefer tactical combat, deep storytelling, or character customization?
2. **Experience Level**: Are your players new to D&D, or are they experienced veterans? Some editions are more beginner-friendly, while others offer more complexity.
3. **Playstyle**: Do you prefer a fast-paced, rules-light game, or do you enjoy detailed mechanics and strategic planning?
4. **Availability**: Which editions are readily available in terms of rulebooks and resources?

Example: Choosing for Your Group

If your group enjoys storytelling and character development, and prefers a streamlined, easy-to-learn system, 5th Edition might be the best choice. If you have a group of experienced players who enjoy tactical combat and complex mechanics, you might consider 3rd Edition or 4th Edition.

Creating Your Character

ELF GNOME HALF ORC DWARF HUMAN HALFLING HALF ELF

Creating a character in Dungeons and Dragons (D&D) is one of the most exciting parts of the game. Your character is your avatar in the game world, and you will guide them through countless adventures, challenges, and growth. This chapter will guide you through understanding character sheets, choosing your race and class, and crafting a character that you will enjoy playing.

Understanding Character Sheets

A character sheet is a crucial tool for keeping track of all the details about your character. It includes information on your character's abilities, skills, equipment, and more. Let's break down each section of a typical character sheet:

Basic Information

This section includes the character's name, race, class, background, player name, alignment, and experience points (XP).

- **Character Name**: The name your character goes by in the game.
- **Race**: The character's species (e.g., human, elf, dwarf).
- **Class**: The character's profession or role (e.g., fighter, wizard, rogue).
- **Background**: The character's life before adventuring (e.g., soldier, noble, scholar).
- **Player Name**: Your name, as the player controlling the character.
- **Alignment**: The character's ethical and moral perspective (e.g., lawful good, chaotic neutral).
- **Experience Points (XP)**: Tracks the character's progress and level advancement.

Example

Elara, a half-elf wizard, has an alignment of neutral good and a background as a sage. Her player, Alex, notes these details in the basic information section.

Ability Scores

Ability scores represent the character's physical and mental attributes. There are six abilities: Strength, Dexterity, Constitution, Intelligence, Wisdom, and Charisma. Each ability score has a modifier that affects related rolls and checks.

- **Strength (STR)**: Physical power and force.
- **Dexterity (DEX)**: Agility, reflexes, and balance.
- **Constitution (CON)**: Health, stamina, and vital force.
- **Intelligence (INT)**: Reasoning and memory.
- **Wisdom (WIS)**: Perception and insight.
- **Charisma (CHA)**: Force of personality, persuasion, and leadership.

Example

Elara has an Intelligence score of 16 (+3 modifier), a Dexterity score of 14 (+2 modifier), and a Constitution score of 12 (+1 modifier). These scores and modifiers are recorded on her character sheet.

Proficiency Bonus

Your proficiency bonus is a number that you add to any roll involving a skill or tool that your character is proficient in. It increases as your character levels up.

Example

At level 1, Elara has a proficiency bonus of +2. As a wizard, she is proficient in Arcana and Investigation, so she adds +2 to rolls involving these skills.

Skills

Skills are specific areas of expertise tied to ability scores. When making a skill check, you add your ability modifier and proficiency bonus (if applicable) to the roll.

Example

Elara's Intelligence modifier is +3, and her proficiency bonus is +2. For an Arcana check, she rolls a d20 and adds +5 (3 from Intelligence and 2 from proficiency).

Saving Throws

Saving throws are checks made to resist or mitigate effects such as spells, traps, or poisons. Each class grants proficiency in two saving throws.

Example

As a wizard, Elara is proficient in Intelligence and Wisdom saving throws. For an Intelligence saving throw, she adds her Intelligence modifier (+3) and proficiency bonus (+2), totaling +5.

Hit Points and Hit Dice

Hit points (HP) represent your character's health and ability to withstand damage. Hit dice are used to determine HP and for healing during rests.

- **Max HP**: The total health points your character has.
- **Current HP**: Your character's current health.
- **Hit Dice**: Used to regain HP during a short rest.

Example

Elara, a level 1 wizard, has 6 hit points (1d6 hit die + her Constitution modifier). She records this on her character sheet, along with the notation that her hit die is 1d6.

Equipment and Inventory

This section lists the items your character carries, including weapons, armor, tools, and other gear. It's important to keep track of weight and encumbrance, as carrying too much can affect your character's movement and abilities.

Example

Elara starts with a spellbook, a component pouch, and basic adventuring gear. She lists these items and their weights on her character sheet.

Features and Traits

This section includes any special abilities or features granted by your race, class, or background. It also covers traits like darkvision, special resistances, or languages known.

Example

Elara, being a half-elf, has darkvision and proficiency in two skills of her choice (History and Investigation). As a wizard, she has the Spellcasting feature, allowing her to cast spells.

Spells

For spellcasting classes, this section details known spells, spell slots, and spell save DCs. It's crucial for keeping track of spells prepared and used during gameplay.

Example

Elara knows three cantrips (Mage Hand, Prestidigitation, Fire Bolt) and has prepared spells like Magic Missile and Shield. She notes her spell save DC (8 + proficiency bonus + Intelligence modifier) and spell attack bonus.

Races and Classes

Choosing a race and class for your character is a critical decision that shapes their abilities, appearance, and role in the game. Each race and class has unique features and traits that provide different advantages and playstyles.

Races

Races determine your character's physical traits, lifespan, abilities, and cultural background. Each race comes with specific bonuses and traits that enhance certain abilities and skills.

Humans

Humans are the most versatile and adaptable race in D&D. They are known for their diversity and ambition.

- **Ability Score Increase**: +1 to all ability scores.
- **Traits**: Extra language, increased versatility.
- **Example**: A human fighter like Sir Cedric benefits from balanced ability scores, making him proficient in various combat and non-combat situations.

Elves

Elves are known for their grace, longevity, and keen senses. They are often attuned to nature and magic.

- **Ability Score Increase**: +2 Dexterity.

- **Traits**: Darkvision, Fey Ancestry, proficiency in Perception.
- **Subraces**: High Elves (extra cantrip, +1 Intelligence), Wood Elves (increased speed, +1 Wisdom), Drow (superior darkvision, +1 Charisma).
- **Example**: Elara, a high elf wizard, benefits from a Dexterity increase for better defense and an Intelligence increase for improved spellcasting.

Dwarves

Dwarves are hardy and resilient, known for their endurance and craftsmanship.

- **Ability Score Increase**: +2 Constitution.
- **Traits**: Darkvision, Dwarven Resilience (resistance to poison), proficiency with certain weapons.
- **Subraces**: Hill Dwarves (+1 Wisdom, extra hit points), Mountain Dwarves (+2 Strength, armor proficiency).
- **Example**: Thrain, a hill dwarf cleric, gains extra hit points and wisdom, making him a robust and insightful healer.

Half-Elves

Half-Elves combine the best traits of humans and elves, offering versatility and charm.

- **Ability Score Increase**: +2 Charisma, +1 to two other ability scores.
- **Traits**: Darkvision, Fey Ancestry, skill versatility (proficiency in two skills).
- **Example**: Elara, a half-elf wizard, enjoys increased Charisma for social interactions and boosts to Intelligence and Dexterity for spellcasting and defense.

Tieflings

Tieflings are known for their infernal heritage, which grants them unique abilities and resistance to fire.

- **Ability Score Increase**: +2 Charisma, +1 Intelligence.
- **Traits**: Darkvision, Hellish Resistance (fire resistance), Infernal Legacy (innate spellcasting).
- **Example**: Kael, a tiefling warlock, uses his increased Charisma for spellcasting and social maneuvers, along with innate spells like Thaumaturgy.

Classes

Classes determine your character's skills, abilities, and role in the party. Each class has unique features, proficiencies, and playstyles.

Fighters

Fighters are masters of combat, skilled with a variety of weapons and armor.

- **Hit Die**: d10.
- **Primary Abilities**: Strength or Dexterity.
- **Saving Throws**: Strength, Constitution.
- **Proficiencies**: All armor, shields, simple and martial weapons.
- **Example**: Sir Cedric, a human fighter, excels in melee combat, using his high Strength for powerful attacks and heavy armor for protection.

Wizards

Wizards are arcane spellcasters who study and wield powerful magic.

- **Hit Die**: d6.
- **Primary Ability**: Intelligence.
- **Saving Throws**: Intelligence, Wisdom.
- **Proficiencies**: Daggers, darts, slings, quarterstaffs, light crossbows.
- **Example**: Elara, a half-elf wizard, uses her high Intelligence to cast powerful spells, relying on her arcane knowledge to control the battlefield.

Rogues

Rogues are agile and cunning, excelling in stealth, thievery, and precision strikes.

- **Hit Die**: d8.
- **Primary Ability**: Dexterity.
- **Saving Throws**: Dexterity, Intelligence.
- **Proficiencies**: Light armor, simple weapons, hand crossbows, longswords, rapiers, shortswords, thieves' tools.
- **Example**: Lira, a halfling rogue, uses her Dexterity for stealth and acrobatics, delivering precise and deadly sneak attacks.

Clerics

Clerics are divine spellcasters who draw power from their deities to heal and protect, as well as to smite their foes.

- **Hit Die**: d8.
- **Primary Ability**: Wisdom.
- **Saving Throws**: Wisdom, Charisma.
- **Proficiencies**: Light and medium armor, shields, simple weapons.
- **Example**: Thrain, a hill dwarf cleric, uses his Wisdom to cast healing and protective spells, supporting his allies in combat.

Crafting Your Character

When crafting your character, consider the following steps:

1. **Concept**: Think about your character's backstory, personality, and motivations. What drives them to adventure?
2. **Race and Class**: Choose a race and class that fit your concept and preferred playstyle.
3. **Ability Scores**: Assign ability scores based on your class's primary abilities and your character's strengths.
4. **Background**: Select a background that provides additional skills, languages, and proficiencies.
5. **Skills and Proficiencies**: Choose skills and tools that enhance your character's abilities and role in the party.
6. **Equipment**: Equip your character with appropriate gear, considering their starting gold and class options.
7. **Spells**: For spellcasters, choose spells that complement your character's abilities and anticipated challenges.
8. **Details**: Fill in the details such as alignment, appearance, personality traits, and bonds.

By carefully crafting your character, you create a unique and engaging persona that enhances your D&D experience. Your character's abilities, personality, and story will shape the adventures and challenges you face, making every game session a memorable journey.

Backgrounds and Alignments

Backgrounds

Backgrounds in Dungeons and Dragons (D&D) provide a foundation for your character's past and influence their skills, proficiencies, and personal history. A well-chosen background adds depth to your character, offering role-playing hooks and potential plot points for your adventures.

Components of a Background

Each background includes the following components:

1. **Skill Proficiencies**: Specific skills your character excels in due to their background.
2. **Tool Proficiencies**: Proficiency with certain tools or instruments relevant to the background.
3. **Languages**: Additional languages your character can speak or understand.
4. **Equipment**: Starting equipment related to the background.
5. **Feature**: A unique ability or advantage provided by the background.

6. **Suggested Characteristics**: Personality traits, ideals, bonds, and flaws to help flesh out your character's personality.

Common Backgrounds

Acolyte

- **Skill Proficiencies**: Insight, Religion.
- **Tool Proficiencies**: None.
- **Languages**: Two of your choice.
- **Equipment**: A holy symbol, prayer book or wheel, 5 sticks of incense, vestments, common clothes, and a pouch with 15 gp.
- **Feature**: Shelter of the Faithful – You and your companions can expect aid from those who share your faith.
- **Example**: A character with the Acolyte background might have been raised in a temple and learned the ways of their deity, providing insight into religious matters and spiritual guidance.

Soldier

- **Skill Proficiencies**: Athletics, Intimidation.
- **Tool Proficiencies**: One type of gaming set, vehicles (land).
- **Languages**: None.

- **Equipment**: An insignia of rank, a trophy from a fallen enemy, a set of bone dice or deck of cards, common clothes, and a pouch with 10 gp.
- **Feature**: Military Rank – Soldiers recognize your authority and defer to your rank.
- **Example**: A character with the Soldier background might have served in an army, giving them skills in combat tactics and leadership, as well as a reputation among other soldiers.

Noble

- **Skill Proficiencies**: History, Persuasion.
- **Tool Proficiencies**: One type of gaming set.
- **Languages**: One of your choice.
- **Equipment**: A set of fine clothes, a signet ring, a scroll of pedigree, and a purse with 25 gp.
- **Feature**: Position of Privilege – People of the lower classes are inclined to defer to you, and you can secure an audience with other nobles.
- **Example**: A character with the Noble background might come from a wealthy and influential family, using their knowledge of history and social skills to navigate high society and political intrigue.

Alignments

Alignment in D&D represents your character's ethical and moral perspective, guiding their actions and decisions. It consists of two components: ethical (Lawful, Neutral, Chaotic) and moral (Good, Neutral, Evil).

Ethical Axis

- **Lawful**: Values order, rules, and structure. Follows a code or set of principles.
- **Neutral**: Balances between order and chaos, adaptable to circumstances.
- **Chaotic**: Values freedom, individuality, and spontaneity. Dislikes restrictions.

Moral Axis

- **Good**: Acts with compassion, altruism, and respect for life.
- **Neutral**: Balances self-interest with the needs of others, without strong leanings toward good or evil.
- **Evil**: Acts with selfishness, cruelty, and disregard for others.

Examples of Alignments

- **Lawful Good (LG)**: Follows a personal code of honor and helps others. Example: A

paladin who fights for justice and protects the innocent.
- **Chaotic Neutral (CN)**: Acts based on personal whims and desires, without regard for law or morality. Example: A rogue who seeks freedom and adventure, caring little for laws or ethics.
- **Neutral Evil (NE)**: Acts purely out of self-interest, willing to harm others for personal gain. Example: A necromancer who raises the dead to build power and wealth.

Abilities and Skills

Ability Scores

Ability scores represent your character's physical and mental attributes. There are six ability scores: Strength, Dexterity, Constitution, Intelligence, Wisdom, and Charisma. These scores affect nearly every aspect of your character's performance in the game.

Ability Score Generation Methods

There are several methods to generate ability scores, each providing a different balance of control and randomness:

1. **Standard Array**: A predefined set of scores (15, 14, 13, 12, 10, 8) that players assign to their abilities.
2. **Point Buy**: Players start with a set number of points to allocate, allowing customization within limits.
3. **Rolling for Scores**: Players roll dice to determine their scores, introducing an element of chance.

Ability Scores and Modifiers

Each ability score has an associated modifier, calculated as (Ability Score - 10) / 2, rounded down. This modifier is added to relevant rolls and checks.

- **Strength (STR)**: Physical power and force. Affects melee attacks, damage, and carrying capacity.
- **Dexterity (DEX)**: Agility, reflexes, and balance. Affects ranged attacks, AC, and initiative.
- **Constitution (CON)**: Health, stamina, and endurance. Affects hit points and concentration checks.
- **Intelligence (INT)**: Reasoning and knowledge. Affects spellcasting for wizards, and skills like Arcana and Investigation.

- **Wisdom (WIS)**: Perception and insight. Affects spellcasting for clerics and druids, and skills like Perception and Survival.
- **Charisma (CHA)**: Force of personality and social influence. Affects spellcasting for sorcerers and bards, and skills like Persuasion and Deception.

Skills

Skills represent specific areas of expertise tied to ability scores. When performing a skill check, you add your ability modifier and proficiency bonus (if applicable) to the roll.

Skill Proficiencies

Proficiency in a skill allows your character to add their proficiency bonus to related checks. Skills are often tied to backgrounds, classes, and races.

Skill List and Examples

- **Acrobatics (DEX)**: Balancing, tumbling, and nimbleness. Example: Walking a tightrope.
- **Animal Handling (WIS)**: Calming and training animals. Example: Soothing a frightened horse.
- **Arcana (INT)**: Knowledge of magic and arcane lore. Example: Identifying a spell.

- **Athletics (STR)**: Physical feats like climbing, jumping, and swimming. Example: Climbing a cliff.
- **Deception (CHA)**: Bluffing, lying, and trickery. Example: Convincing a guard with a false story.
- **History (INT)**: Knowledge of past events and civilizations. Example: Recalling details of an ancient war.
- **Insight (WIS)**: Reading people and situations. Example: Detecting lies or motives.
- **Intimidation (CHA)**: Coercing or frightening others. Example: Threatening a bandit into submission.
- **Investigation (INT)**: Finding clues and solving mysteries. Example: Examining a crime scene.
- **Medicine (WIS)**: Diagnosing and treating injuries and illnesses. Example: Stabilizing a dying ally.
- **Nature (INT)**: Understanding natural phenomena and creatures. Example: Identifying a plant species.
- **Perception (WIS)**: Noticing details and sensory awareness. Example: Spotting a hidden door.
- **Performance (CHA)**: Entertaining through music, dance, or acting. Example: Singing in a tavern.

- **Persuasion (CHA)**: Influencing others through diplomacy and charm. Example: Negotiating a peace treaty.
- **Religion (INT)**: Knowledge of deities, rituals, and religious lore. Example: Recognizing a holy symbol.
- **Sleight of Hand (DEX)**: Manual dexterity for tricks and theft. Example: Picking a pocket.
- **Stealth (DEX)**: Moving silently and unseen. Example: Sneaking past guards.
- **Survival (WIS)**: Skills for wilderness survival. Example: Tracking a creature or finding food.

Example of Skill Use

Elara, a half-elf wizard with proficiency in Arcana, might roll a d20 and add her Intelligence modifier (+3) and proficiency bonus (+2) to identify a magical artifact. If she rolls a 14 on the d20, her total check would be 19 (14 + 3 + 2), allowing her to recognize the artifact's properties.

Combining Abilities and Skills

Your character's abilities and skills work together to define their capabilities and playstyle. When creating your character, consider how their background, race, class, and abilities align to form a cohesive and effective adventurer.

Example: Creating a Well-Rounded Character

Lira, a halfling rogue, might have the following ability scores and skills:

- **Strength (STR)**: 10 (+0)
- **Dexterity (DEX)**: 16 (+3)
- **Constitution (CON)**: 12 (+1)
- **Intelligence (INT)**: 14 (+2)
- **Wisdom (WIS)**: 13 (+1)
- **Charisma (CHA)**: 15 (+2)

Lira's high Dexterity and proficiency in Stealth and Acrobatics make her an agile and elusive character, while her Intelligence and proficiency in Investigation allow her to solve puzzles and uncover secrets. Her background as a spy might provide additional proficiencies in Deception and Insight, making her adept at gathering information and reading people.

By understanding the interplay between abilities and skills, you can create a character that excels in their chosen role and enriches the group's adventures. Each decision you make, from background to ability scores, shapes your character's journey and contributions to the story.

Understanding the Game Mechanics

Dice and Their Uses

The Polyhedral Dice Set

Dungeons and Dragons (D&D) utilizes a variety of polyhedral dice to determine the outcomes of actions, resolve combat, and navigate complex interactions. The standard dice set includes:

- **d4**: A four-sided die, resembling a pyramid.
- **d6**: A six-sided die, the classic cube.
- **d8**: An eight-sided die.
- **d10**: A ten-sided die, often used for percentile rolls (d100).
- **d12**: A twelve-sided die.
- **d20**: A twenty-sided die, the most iconic in D&D.

Uses of Different Dice

d20 - The Core Mechanic

The d20 is the cornerstone of D&D's game mechanics, used for the majority of checks and resolutions. This system is often referred to as the d20 System. Here's how it works:

1. **Ability Checks**: To determine success or failure in tasks that rely on your character's abilities. Roll a d20 and add the relevant ability modifier and proficiency bonus if applicable. Compare the total to the Difficulty Class (DC) set by the Dungeon Master (DM). For example, if Lira the rogue tries to pick a lock (Dexterity check), she rolls a d20, adds her Dexterity modifier (+3), and her proficiency bonus (+2), aiming to meet or exceed the DC (e.g., DC 15).
2. **Attack Rolls**: To determine if an attack hits. Roll a d20 and add the appropriate modifiers (ability modifier, proficiency bonus). Compare the result to the target's Armor Class (AC). For example, Thrain the cleric swings his mace (Strength-based attack). He rolls a d20, adds his Strength modifier (+2) and proficiency bonus (+2). If his total meets or exceeds the opponent's AC (e.g., AC 14), he hits.
3. **Saving Throws**: To resist effects like spells, poisons, or other hazards. Roll a d20, add the relevant ability modifier and proficiency

bonus if applicable. Compare the result to the DC set by the source of the effect.

d4, d6, d8, d10, d12 - Damage and Random Determinations

These dice are primarily used to determine damage and other variable outcomes:

1. **Damage Rolls**: Different weapons and spells use different dice to calculate damage. For instance, a longsword might deal 1d8 damage, while a fireball spell might deal 8d6 damage. The die rolled depends on the weapon, spell, or effect.
2. **Hit Points**: Character and monster hit points (HP) can be determined using various dice. For example, a wizard might gain 1d6 HP per level, while a barbarian might gain 1d12 HP per level.
3. **Random Effects**: Some spells and abilities require random determinations. For instance, the "Chaos Bolt" spell's damage type is determined by rolling a d8.

d10 (Percentile Dice)

Percentile rolls (d100) involve rolling two ten-sided dice, one representing the tens place and the other the ones place, to produce a result between 01 and

100. This is often used for determining random events or loot.

Examples and Applications

- **Combat Example**: Elara the wizard casts a Magic Missile spell, which always hits and deals 1d4+1 force damage per missile. She rolls three d4s (one for each missile) and adds 1 to each result, totaling the damage.
- **Skill Check Example**: Lira the rogue wants to sneak past a guard. The DM sets the Stealth check DC at 15. Lira rolls a d20, adds her Dexterity modifier (+3), and her proficiency bonus (+2). If she rolls a 10, her total is 15, just enough to succeed.

Understanding the uses of different dice and the d20 system is crucial for playing D&D, as it underpins the game's mechanics and ensures fair and exciting gameplay.

Turn Order and Combat

Initiative and Turn Order

Combat in D&D is structured in rounds, with each round representing six seconds of in-game time. Within each round, all characters and creatures act in a specific order determined by their initiative.

Initiative

1. **Rolling for Initiative**: At the start of combat, each participant rolls a d20 and adds their Dexterity modifier. The DM records these results to determine the order of turns. For example, if Lira rolls a 15 and has a +3 Dexterity modifier, her initiative score is 18.
2. **Initiative Ties**: If two participants have the same initiative score, the DM can decide the order based on house rules, rerolling, or comparing Dexterity scores.

Structure of a Turn

On a character's turn, they can perform a variety of actions. A turn typically consists of:

1. **Movement**: Each character has a movement speed, usually determined by their race (e.g., 30 feet for humans). They can move up to this distance on their turn, splitting it before and after actions if desired.
2. **Action**: The primary activity a character can perform, such as attacking, casting a spell, or using an item. Common actions include:
    - **Attack**: Making a melee or ranged attack.
    - **Cast a Spell**: Casting a spell with a casting time of one action.

- **Dash**: Doubling movement for the turn.
- **Disengage**: Avoiding opportunity attacks for the rest of the turn.
- **Dodge**: Focusing on defense to impose disadvantage on attacks against you.
- **Help**: Granting an ally advantage on their next ability check or attack roll.
- **Use an Object**: Interacting with an object or item.
3. **Bonus Action**: Certain abilities, spells, and features allow additional actions. For example, rogues can use Cunning Action to Dash, Disengage, or Hide as a bonus action.
4. **Reaction**: A special action taken outside of your turn, usually triggered by specific conditions. For example, casting the "Shield" spell when attacked.
5. **Free Actions**: Minor activities that don't require an action, such as talking or drawing a weapon.

Combat Mechanics

Making an Attack

1. **Attack Roll**: Roll a d20 and add the relevant modifiers (ability modifier,

proficiency bonus). Compare the result to the target's AC.
- **Melee Attack**: Uses Strength modifier (or Dexterity for finesse weapons).
- **Ranged Attack**: Uses Dexterity modifier.
2. **Determining Hits**: If the attack roll meets or exceeds the target's AC, the attack hits. Otherwise, it misses.
3. **Damage Roll**: Roll the appropriate dice for the weapon or spell, add relevant modifiers (e.g., Strength for melee weapons), and subtract the result from the target's HP.
4. **Critical Hits**: Rolling a natural 20 on the d20 results in a critical hit, doubling the damage dice rolled.

Example of Combat Round

- **Initiative**: Thrain (17), Elara (15), Lira (18), Orc (12).
- **Lira's Turn**: Lira moves 20 feet to flank an orc. She attacks with her shortsword (d20 + 5). She rolls a 16, hitting the orc (AC 13). She rolls 1d6+3 for damage, dealing 7 damage.
- **Thrain's Turn**: Thrain moves 15 feet to a wounded ally and uses his action to cast "Cure Wounds," healing 1d8+3 HP.

- **Elara's Turn**: Elara casts "Magic Missile," rolling three d4s for 3 missiles, each dealing 1d4+1 damage. She rolls 3, 2, and 4, totaling 13 damage to the orc.
- **Orc's Turn**: The orc swings its greataxe at Lira, rolling a d20 + 5. It rolls a 14, hitting Lira (AC 13). The orc rolls 1d12+3 for damage, dealing 8 damage.

Special Combat Rules

1. **Flanking**: Provides advantage on attack rolls when attacking an enemy from opposite sides with an ally.
2. **Cover**: Objects and obstacles can provide cover, improving AC and saving throws.
    - **Half Cover**: +2 to AC and Dexterity saving throws.
    - **Three-Quarters Cover**: +5 to AC and Dexterity saving throws.
    - **Full Cover**: Cannot be targeted directly by attacks or spells.
3. **Opportunity Attacks**: Leaving an enemy's reach without using the Disengage action provokes an opportunity attack.

Advanced Combat Tactics

1. **Grappling**: Replacing an attack to attempt to grapple, using Athletics (Strength) against the target's Athletics or Acrobatics.
2. **Shoving**: Replacing an attack to push a target, using Athletics (Strength) against the target's Athletics or Acrobatics.
3. **Mounted Combat**: Special rules for fighting on mounts, including controlling the mount and making attacks.

Understanding turn order and combat mechanics is essential for effectively participating in D&D battles. Mastery of these rules allows players to make strategic decisions, coordinate with allies, and overcome the myriad challenges posed by the DM.

Magic and Spellcasting

Magic is a fundamental aspect of Dungeons & Dragons (D&D), allowing characters to wield extraordinary powers. Understanding the mechanics of magic and spellcasting is crucial for players who choose spellcasting classes. This section provides an in-depth breakdown of the key concepts, components, and rules governing magic in D&D.

Magic and Spellcasting

Spellcasting Classes

Spellcasting in D&D is primarily tied to specific classes. Each class has its unique way of accessing and using magic. Here are the primary spellcasting classes:

- **Wizard**: Masters of arcane knowledge who learn spells from spellbooks.
- **Sorcerer**: Innate spellcasters who draw power from their bloodline or other innate sources.
- **Cleric**: Divine spellcasters who receive their magic from deities.
- **Druid**: Nature-based spellcasters who draw power from the natural world.
- **Bard**: Charismatic performers who use music and lore to cast spells.
- **Warlock**: Spellcasters who gain their powers through pacts with powerful beings.
- **Paladin**: Holy warriors who channel divine magic through their oath.
- **Ranger**: Wilderness explorers who use a limited selection of spells to enhance their abilities.

Spell Levels and Spell Slots

Spells are divided into levels from 0 (cantrips) to 9. Higher-level spells are generally more powerful and require higher-level spell slots to cast.

Cantrips

- **Cantrips**: Level 0 spells that do not consume spell slots. Spellcasters can cast these spells at will. Example: "Fire Bolt" (wizard), "Sacred Flame" (cleric).

Spell Slots

- **Spell Slots**: Represent the number of spells a spellcaster can cast at each level per day. Each class has a unique progression of spell slots. For example, a 1st-level wizard has two 1st-level spell slots.

Example of Spell Slots

A 5th-level sorcerer might have the following spell slots:

- Four 1st-level slots
- Three 2nd-level slots
- Two 3rd-level slots

Preparing and Casting Spells

Preparing Spells

Some classes, like wizards and clerics, must prepare spells from their spellbooks or known spells each day. The number of spells they can prepare is typically equal to their class level plus their spellcasting ability modifier.

- **Example**: A 5th-level wizard with an Intelligence modifier of +3 can prepare 8 spells (5 + 3).

Casting Spells

To cast a spell, a spellcaster must expend a spell slot of the spell's level or higher. They must also meet the requirements for casting, such as verbal, somatic, and material components.

- **Verbal (V)**: The spell requires chanting or speaking magic words.
- **Somatic (S)**: The spell requires specific hand gestures.
- **Material (M)**: The spell requires specific items or focus.

Spell Components and Focuses

Material Components

Some spells require specific materials to cast. These can range from simple items like a feather to more exotic components like a diamond worth 1,000 gp.

- **Example**: The "Identify" spell requires a pearl worth at least 100 gp and an owl feather.

Spell Focuses

Spellcasters can use a spell focus (e.g., a wand, staff, holy symbol) to replace material components that do not have a specified cost.

- **Example**: A cleric might use a holy symbol as a spell focus to cast spells without needing specific material components.

Concentration

Some spells require concentration to maintain their effects. A spellcaster can only concentrate on one spell at a time, and taking damage or being incapacitated can force a concentration check (Constitution saving throw) to maintain the spell.

- **Example**: The "Invisibility" spell requires concentration, meaning if the caster takes damage, they must succeed on a Constitution saving throw (DC equal to 10 or half the damage taken, whichever is higher) to maintain the spell.

Ritual Casting

Some spells can be cast as rituals, which do not consume spell slots but take longer to cast (usually 10 additional minutes).

- **Example**: The "Detect Magic" spell can be cast as a ritual, allowing the caster to use it without expending a spell slot.

Example of Spellcasting

Elara, a 5th-level wizard, prepares her spells for the day. She has an Intelligence modifier of +4, allowing her to prepare 9 spells (5 + 4). She chooses the following spells:

1. **Cantrips** (cast at will): Fire Bolt, Mage Hand, Prestidigitation
2. **1st-Level Spells**: Magic Missile, Shield, Detect Magic
3. **2nd-Level Spells**: Invisibility, Mirror Image
4. **3rd-Level Spells**: Fireball, Counterspell

During an encounter, Elara decides to cast Fireball at a group of enemies. She uses one of her two 3rd-level spell slots to cast the spell, rolling 8d6 for damage and targeting the enemies within a 20-foot radius.

Experience and Leveling Up

Experience Points (XP)

Experience Points (XP) are a measure of a character's progression and growth. Characters earn XP by defeating monsters, completing quests, and achieving significant milestones in the game.

Awarding XP

The Dungeon Master (DM) determines how much XP to award based on the challenge and significance of encounters and achievements. XP can be awarded individually or divided among the party.

- **Example**: A party of four characters defeats a group of goblins worth 400 XP total. Each character receives 100 XP.

Leveling Up

When a character accumulates enough XP, they level up, gaining new abilities, spells, and improvements to their statistics.

Level Progression

Each class has a unique progression table that outlines the XP needed for each level and the benefits gained. For example, a wizard might gain new spell slots and spells known, while a fighter might gain additional attacks and combat abilities.

Benefits of Leveling Up

1. **Ability Score Improvements (ASIs)**: At certain levels, characters can increase their ability scores or choose a feat to enhance their capabilities.
2. **Hit Points**: Characters gain additional hit points based on their class's hit dice and Constitution modifier.
3. **New Abilities and Spells**: Depending on the class, characters gain new features, abilities, and spells.
4. **Proficiency Bonus**: Increases at certain levels, improving attack rolls, saving throws, and skill checks.

Example of Leveling Up

Lira, a 4th-level rogue, earns enough XP to reach 5th level. Here's how she levels up:

1. **Hit Points**: She rolls her hit dice (1d8) and adds her Constitution modifier (+2). She rolls a 6, so her hit points increase by 8 (6 + 2).
2. **Sneak Attack**: Her Sneak Attack damage increases from 2d6 to 3d6.
3. **Uncanny Dodge**: She gains the Uncanny Dodge feature, allowing her to use her reaction to halve the damage of an attack she can see.
4. **Ability Score Improvement**: She chooses to increase her Dexterity by 2, raising her

Dexterity score from 16 to 18, which also increases her Dexterity modifier from +3 to +4.

Milestone Leveling

Some DMs use milestone leveling instead of tracking XP. In this system, characters level up based on significant story events, accomplishments, and plot progression.

- **Example**: After completing a major quest to retrieve an ancient artifact, the DM decides the party has reached a milestone and grants them a level up.

Playing the Game

Roleplaying Basics

Understanding Roleplaying

Roleplaying is at the heart of Dungeons & Dragons (D&D), allowing players to immerse themselves in their characters and the game world. It involves acting, decision-making, and interacting as your character would, contributing to the collaborative storytelling experience.

Key Aspects of Roleplaying

1. **Character Development**: Embrace your character's background, personality, and motivations. Think about how they would react to various situations, what drives them, and how they interact with others.
2. **Narrative Contribution**: Your roleplaying contributes to the overall narrative. Collaborate with the Dungeon Master (DM)

and other players to weave a compelling story.
3. **Immersion**: Stay in character as much as possible. Use your character's voice, mannerisms, and perspectives to enhance the game's immersion.

Example of Roleplaying

Lira the rogue has a background as a spy. She's cautious, calculating, and distrustful of authority. When the party meets a suspicious noble, Lira might choose to hang back, observe quietly, and gather information before making any moves.

Creating a Character Persona

To effectively roleplay, develop a detailed persona for your character. Consider these elements:

1. **Background**: Where did your character come from? What past experiences shaped them?
2. **Personality**: What are their key traits? Are they brave, cunning, compassionate, or ruthless?
3. **Goals and Motivations**: What drives your character? What do they hope to achieve?
4. **Relationships**: How does your character relate to others in the party and the world?

Example of Character Persona

Thrain the cleric is a devout follower of a god of justice. He's honorable, dedicated, and unyielding in his quest to root out evil. His goal is to cleanse the land of corruption and protect the innocent. Thrain's stern demeanor can be off-putting, but his loyalty to his friends is unwavering.

Interactions and Social Encounters

Social encounters in D&D are opportunities for characters to interact with non-player characters (NPCs) and each other. These encounters can drive the plot, provide crucial information, and offer opportunities for roleplaying and problem-solving.

Types of Social Encounters

1. **Information Gathering**: Characters seek information from NPCs, such as clues, rumors, or directions.
2. **Negotiation**: Characters negotiate for resources, alliances, or peace.
3. **Deception and Persuasion**: Characters use their charisma and skills to deceive, persuade, or intimidate NPCs.
4. **Conflict Resolution**: Characters resolve conflicts through dialogue rather than combat.

Conducting Social Encounters

Social encounters typically involve a combination of roleplaying and skill checks. The DM sets the scene, describes the NPCs, and guides the interaction. Players respond in character, using dialogue and actions to achieve their goals.

Role of the DM

The DM plays all NPCs, describing their appearance, behavior, and reactions. The DM also determines the difficulty of social challenges and decides when to call for skill checks.

Key Skills for Social Encounters

1. **Persuasion**: Convincing NPCs to agree with you or do something for you.
   - **Example**: Elara the wizard uses Persuasion to convince a guard to let the party pass without proper papers. She rolls a d20, adds her Charisma modifier (+2), and her proficiency bonus (+2), aiming to meet the guard's DC of 15.
2. **Deception**: Lying or misleading NPCs.
   - **Example**: Lira the rogue tries to deceive a merchant into thinking a fake gem is real. She rolls a d20, adds her Charisma modifier (+3) and

proficiency bonus (+2), aiming to meet the merchant's DC of 14.
3. **Intimidation**: Using threats or forceful presence to influence NPCs.
    - **Example**: Thrain the cleric uses Intimidation to make a bandit reveal his hideout. He rolls a d20, adds his Strength modifier (+3) and proficiency bonus (+2), aiming to meet the bandit's DC of 13.
4. **Insight**: Reading NPCs' intentions, detecting lies, or understanding their emotions.
    - **Example**: Thrain suspects a noble of hiding something. He rolls a d20, adds his Wisdom modifier (+3) and proficiency bonus (+2), aiming to meet the DC set by the noble's Deception roll.

Examples of Social Encounters

Information Gathering

The party enters a bustling tavern looking for information about a missing person. The DM describes the scene: patrons drinking, chatting, and a bard playing music. Elara decides to approach the barkeep.

Elara: "Good evening. I'm looking for a friend who might have passed through here. Have you seen a man in a red cloak?"

DM: "The barkeep narrows his eyes. 'Maybe I have, maybe I haven't. What's it worth to you?'"

Elara decides to use Persuasion. She rolls a d20, adds her Charisma modifier (+2) and proficiency bonus (+2), totaling 18. The DM sets the DC at 15, so she succeeds.

DM: "The barkeep leans in. 'Alright, I did see someone like that. He was asking about a place called Raven's Hollow.'"

Negotiation

The party needs to cross a bridge controlled by a rival faction. Lira, the party's negotiator, steps forward to speak with the faction leader.

Lira: "We need safe passage across the bridge. In return, we can offer you valuable information about your enemies' movements."

The DM decides this requires a Persuasion check and sets the DC at 16. Lira rolls a d20, adds her Charisma modifier (+3) and proficiency bonus (+2), totaling 19.

DM: "The leader strokes his chin. 'Very well. You may pass, but if your information is false, you will answer to me.'"

Deception

The party wants to avoid a confrontation with a group of guards. Thrain decides to bluff their way out.

Thrain: "We're on official business from the king. Step aside!"

The DM sets the DC at 14. Thrain rolls a d20, adds his Charisma modifier (+1) and proficiency bonus (+2), totaling 15.

DM: "The guards glance at each other nervously. 'Alright, move along. But we'll be watching you.'"

Conflict Resolution

Two rival factions are about to clash in the marketplace. Elara steps forward to mediate.

Elara: "Hold! This fighting will only bring more trouble. Let's find a peaceful solution."

The DM calls for a Persuasion check with a DC of 18. Elara rolls a d20, adds her Charisma modifier (+2) and proficiency bonus (+2), totaling 17, failing the check.

DM: "The tension is too high. One of the faction leaders shouts, 'Get out of the way, or you'll be next!' The crowd erupts into chaos."

Enhancing Roleplaying in Social Encounters

In-Character Dialogue

Speak as your character would. Use their voice, mannerisms, and vocabulary to bring them to life.

- **Example**: Thrain speaks with a stern, authoritative tone, reflecting his role as a cleric of justice.

Descriptive Actions

Describe your character's actions and expressions. This helps paint a vivid picture for other players and the DM.

- **Example**: Lira narrows her eyes, scanning the room for hidden threats. Her fingers twitch near her dagger, ready for action.

Engaging with NPCs

Treat NPCs as real characters with their own motivations and personalities. Build relationships, make allies, and create conflicts.

- **Example**: Elara befriends a local scholar, exchanging knowledge and gaining a valuable ally in the city.

Final Thoughts on Social Encounters

Social encounters are a vital part of D&D, offering opportunities for roleplaying, problem-solving, and advancing the story. By understanding the mechanics and embracing your character's persona, you can navigate these interactions effectively and contribute to the game's rich narrative. Whether you're gathering information, negotiating alliances, or deceiving foes, your actions and decisions shape the world and the unfolding adventure.

Exploration and Quests

The Importance of Exploration

Exploration in Dungeons & Dragons (D&D) is about discovering new places, uncovering secrets, and interacting with the environment. It's a crucial aspect of the game that complements combat and social encounters, enriching the overall experience. Exploration can lead to finding hidden treasures, learning about the game world, and encountering unexpected challenges.

Components of Exploration

1. **Overland Travel**: Moving from one location to another, often involving navigating terrain, facing natural hazards, and managing resources.
2. **Dungeon Delving**: Exploring ancient ruins, hidden dungeons, and mysterious places filled with traps, puzzles, and enemies.
3. **Urban Exploration**: Investigating cities and towns, interacting with local NPCs, and uncovering secrets hidden within urban settings.

Overland Travel

Overland travel involves moving across different terrains such as forests, mountains, and deserts. The DM describes the environment, and players decide their path and actions.

Key Considerations

1. **Navigation**: Using skills like Survival to find the best route and avoid getting lost.
2. **Resources**: Managing food, water, and supplies for the journey.
3. **Encounters**: Facing random or planned encounters with creatures, NPCs, or environmental hazards.

Example of Overland Travel

The party needs to travel through a dense forest to reach a distant city. The DM describes the forest as thick with underbrush and teeming with wildlife. Lira, the rogue, uses her Survival skill to navigate the terrain.

Lira: "I'll scout ahead to find a clear path."

The DM sets the DC at 15. Lira rolls a d20, adds her Wisdom modifier (+2) and proficiency bonus (+2), totaling 18.

DM: "You find a narrow game trail that looks frequently used. It should make the journey easier."

Dungeon Delving

Dungeons are a staple of D&D, offering a mix of combat, puzzles, and exploration. Delving into a dungeon requires caution and strategy.

Key Elements

1. **Mapping**: Keeping track of the party's location within the dungeon to avoid getting lost.
2. **Traps and Hazards**: Detecting and disarming traps using skills like Perception and Thieves' Tools.
3. **Puzzles and Riddles**: Solving challenges that require creative thinking and teamwork.

Example of Dungeon Delving

The party explores an ancient tomb rumored to hold a powerful artifact. The DM describes a dark, musty hallway with faded murals on the walls.

Thrain: "I'll check for traps along the floor."

The DM sets the DC at 14. Thrain rolls a d20, adds his Wisdom modifier (+3) and proficiency bonus (+2), totaling 17.

DM: "You find a pressure plate and carefully disable it. You proceed safely."

Urban Exploration

Urban exploration involves navigating cities and towns, gathering information, and interacting with various NPCs. It's an opportunity to delve into the social and political fabric of the game world.

Key Activities

1. **Information Gathering**: Talking to locals, visiting libraries, and eavesdropping on conversations to learn about the city's secrets.
2. **Investigations**: Solving mysteries, following leads, and uncovering hidden plots.

3. **Commerce**: Buying and selling goods, negotiating with merchants, and commissioning custom items.

Example of Urban Exploration

The party arrives in a bustling port city to find a missing person. The DM describes the busy docks, filled with sailors and merchants.

Elara: "I'll visit the local tavern to gather information."

The DM sets the DC at 13 for a Persuasion check. Elara rolls a d20, adds her Charisma modifier (+2) and proficiency bonus (+2), totaling 16.

DM: "A sailor mentions seeing someone matching your description heading to the warehouse district."

Quests

Quests are the driving force behind the game's narrative, providing goals and motivation for the party. They range from simple tasks to epic adventures.

Types of Quests

1. **Fetch Quests**: Simple tasks involving retrieving an item or delivering a message.

2. **Rescue Missions**: Saving a captured NPC or liberating a besieged town.
3. **Investigations**: Solving mysteries, uncovering hidden truths, and piecing together clues.
4. **Epic Campaigns**: Long-term quests that span multiple sessions, involving significant stakes and challenges.

Structuring Quests

1. **Objectives**: Clear goals for the party to achieve.
2. **Obstacles**: Challenges and adversaries that stand in the way.
3. **Rewards**: Incentives for completing the quest, such as gold, magical items, and XP.

Example of a Quest

Quest Name: The Lost Heirloom

Objective: Retrieve a stolen family heirloom from a bandit camp.

Obstacles: Navigate through a dense forest, defeat the bandits, and disarm traps in the bandit leader's lair.

Rewards: 500 gold pieces, a magical weapon, and a favor from the noble family.

DM: "A local noble approaches you with a plea. 'My family's heirloom has been stolen by bandits. Will you help us retrieve it?'"

Party: "We accept!"

DM: "You set off into the forest, facing dangers along the way."

Combat Strategies

Combat in D&D is tactical and requires strategic thinking to overcome adversaries. Understanding the mechanics and developing effective strategies can make the difference between victory and defeat.

Understanding Combat Mechanics

1. **Initiative**: Determines the order of actions in combat. Players roll a d20 and add their Dexterity modifier.
2. **Actions**: On their turn, characters can take actions such as Attack, Cast a Spell, or Use an Object.
3. **Movement**: Characters can move up to their speed on their turn, including taking specific movement actions like Dash or Disengage.
4. **Bonus Actions**: Certain abilities and spells allow for an additional action on the character's turn.

5. **Reactions**: Responses to specific triggers, such as making an opportunity attack when an enemy leaves your reach.

Key Strategies

1. **Positioning**: Utilize the battlefield's terrain to your advantage. Take cover, avoid clumping together, and flank enemies for tactical benefits.
2. **Focus Fire**: Concentrate attacks on priority targets to quickly reduce the number of threats.
3. **Crowd Control**: Use spells and abilities to control the battlefield, such as "Hold Person" to paralyze an enemy or "Web" to create difficult terrain.
4. **Healing and Buffing**: Support allies by healing wounds and enhancing their abilities with spells like "Cure Wounds" or "Bless."
5. **Resource Management**: Conserve limited resources such as spell slots, potions, and special abilities for critical moments.

Example of Combat Strategies

Positioning

The party faces a group of goblins in a forest clearing. Thrain, the cleric, positions himself behind a large rock for cover, reducing the chance of being hit by ranged attacks.

Thrain: "I take cover behind the rock and prepare to cast a spell."

Focus Fire

The goblin leader is the most dangerous enemy, capable of rallying the other goblins and dealing significant damage. The party decides to focus their attacks on him first.

Lira: "I aim my bow at the goblin leader and fire."

The party coordinates their attacks, quickly taking down the leader and causing the remaining goblins to scatter.

Crowd Control

Elara, the wizard, casts "Sleep" on a group of advancing goblins, putting several to sleep and reducing the immediate threat.

Elara: "I cast Sleep on the goblins in front of us."

The DM rolls 5d8, totaling 23 hit points worth of creatures put to sleep. Three goblins fall unconscious, allowing the party to focus on the remaining enemies.

Healing and Buffing

Thrain casts "Cure Wounds" on Lira, who was injured in the battle, restoring her hit points and keeping her in the fight.

Thrain: "I cast Cure Wounds on Lira, healing her for 1d8 + 3."

The DM rolls a 6, adding Thrain's Wisdom modifier (+3) for a total of 9 hit points restored.

Resource Management

Elara has limited spell slots and decides to save her higher-level spells for potential tougher encounters later. She uses a cantrip, "Fire Bolt," to deal damage without expending a spell slot.

Elara: "I cast Fire Bolt at the nearest goblin."

She rolls a d20, adds her spell attack modifier (+5), and hits the goblin, rolling 1d10 for damage.

Tactical Coordination

Effective combat often involves coordination between party members. Discussing strategies and planning moves can lead to more efficient and successful encounters.

Example of Tactical Coordination

The party faces a group of orcs blocking their path in a narrow canyon. They decide on a plan:

1. **Thrain**: Uses "Shield of Faith" to boost the party's AC.
2. **Elara**: Casts "Web" to restrict the orcs' movement.
3. **Lira**: Uses her bonus action to hide, then attacks from stealth for extra damage.
4. **Party**: Focuses fire on the orc leader to disrupt their command structure.

By coordinating their actions, the party can control the battlefield, reduce incoming damage, and defeat the orcs efficiently.

Dungeon Mastering

Role of the Dungeon Master

The Responsibilities of the Dungeon Master

The Dungeon Master (DM) is the cornerstone of any Dungeons & Dragons (D&D) game. The DM creates and manages the game world, narrates the story, controls non-player characters (NPCs), adjudicates rules, and ensures the game runs smoothly. Here's an in-depth look at the various responsibilities of a DM:

Storytelling

1. **Narration**: The DM describes the settings, scenes, and actions, bringing the game world to life for the players. This includes everything from the weather and landscape to the ambiance of a bustling tavern or the eerie silence of a haunted forest.
2. **Plot Development**: The DM crafts the overarching plot and the subplots that weave

through the campaign. This involves creating engaging storylines, surprising twists, and memorable climaxes.
3. **Character Integration**: Incorporating player characters' backstories and goals into the campaign to make the story personal and engaging for each player.

World-Building

1. **Setting Creation**: Designing the world, including its geography, cultures, politics, history, and mythology. This can be an entirely original world or an adaptation of an existing one.
2. **NPCs**: Creating and roleplaying NPCs, giving them distinct personalities, voices, and motivations. These characters populate the world and interact with the player characters.
3. **Environments**: Detailing locations where the adventure takes place, from sprawling cities and ancient ruins to enchanted forests and treacherous dungeons.

Rule Adjudication

1. **Understanding the Rules**: Familiarity with the rules of the chosen edition of D&D is crucial. The DM must interpret and enforce these rules during gameplay.

2. **Fairness and Flexibility**: Balancing adherence to the rules with flexibility to maintain the flow of the game and the enjoyment of the players. Sometimes this means making on-the-fly rulings or adjusting challenges to fit the narrative.
3. **Conflict Resolution**: Handling disputes or disagreements at the table, ensuring a fair and enjoyable experience for all players.

Game Management

1. **Pacing**: Managing the pacing of the game, balancing combat, exploration, and social encounters to keep the game engaging and dynamic.
2. **Player Engagement**: Keeping players involved and invested in the story. This involves encouraging roleplaying, ensuring everyone has a chance to contribute, and addressing any issues that arise.
3. **Session Preparation**: Planning and organizing game sessions, including preparing encounters, maps, and any necessary props or handouts.

Example of DM Responsibilities

Scene Setting: The DM describes a dark forest where the party has set up camp for the night. The DM narrates the sounds of nocturnal creatures, the flickering light of the campfire, and the rustling of leaves in the wind.

Plot Twist: The party finds a clue leading them to believe a trusted ally might be a double agent. The DM had planned this twist as part of the overarching plot to keep players on their toes.

NPC Roleplay: The DM plays the role of a grizzled old merchant in a bustling marketplace, complete with a gravelly voice and a penchant for tall tales, making the interaction memorable for the players.

Preparing Your Campaign

Campaign Planning

Campaign planning involves creating a structured, yet flexible, framework for the story and adventures your players will experience. This section delves into the detailed steps and considerations for planning a campaign.

Setting the Stage

1. **Choosing the Setting**: Decide whether to use a published setting (like the Forgotten Realms or Eberron) or create your own. Consider the type of world that best suits your story and players' interests.

2. **World Building**: Flesh out the setting's geography, cultures, politics, and history. Create a coherent and immersive world that feels alive and dynamic.
3. **Theme and Tone**: Determine the overarching theme and tone of your campaign. Will it be dark and gritty, light-hearted and whimsical, or something else entirely?

Example of Setting the Stage

The DM decides to set the campaign in the Forgotten Realms, a classic D&D setting. The campaign will focus on the Sword Coast, a region known for its diverse cultures, political intrigue, and ancient ruins. The theme will be a mix of high adventure and political intrigue, with a tone that balances serious challenges with moments of humor and camaraderie.

Crafting the Plot

1. **Main Storyline**: Develop the central plot of the campaign. This could be an epic quest to stop a rising dark power, a mystery to uncover hidden truths, or a series of connected adventures.
2. **Subplots and Side Quests**: Create secondary storylines and optional quests to

enrich the main plot and provide players with choices and additional content.
3. **Character Integration**: Weave player characters' backstories and goals into the main plot and subplots, making their personal stories an integral part of the campaign.

Example of Crafting the Plot

The main storyline involves an ancient prophecy foretelling the return of a long-banished evil. The party must gather ancient artifacts to prevent the prophecy from coming true. Subplots include political intrigue in the city of Waterdeep, a lost heir seeking to reclaim their throne, and a dragon cult causing havoc in the countryside. Each player character has ties to these events, whether through their backgrounds or personal goals.

Designing Encounters

1. **Combat Encounters**: Plan battles that challenge the party and fit within the narrative. Consider the balance between difficulty and enjoyment.
2. **Social Encounters**: Create opportunities for roleplaying and interaction with NPCs. These encounters can provide information, forge alliances, or present moral dilemmas.

3. **Exploration Encounters**: Design areas for the party to explore, filled with traps, puzzles, and hidden treasures. Ensure these encounters contribute to the story and provide meaningful challenges.

Example of Designing Encounters

For a session, the DM plans a combat encounter with a band of orc raiders attacking a village. A social encounter follows where the party negotiates with the village leader for information about the raiders' base. The exploration encounter involves navigating an ancient forest filled with traps set by the orcs to deter pursuers.

Preparing Session Materials

1. **Session Outline**: Create a rough outline of the session, including key encounters, locations, and plot points. Be flexible to adjust based on player actions.
2. **Maps and Props**: Prepare any necessary maps, whether hand-drawn or digital. Props like letters, artifacts, or tokens can enhance the experience.
3. **NPC Details**: Write brief descriptions and motivations for NPCs the party will encounter. This helps maintain consistency and depth in roleplaying.

Example of Preparing Session Materials

For the upcoming session, the DM prepares a map of the village under attack, including the orc raiders' positions. The DM also writes short descriptions for the village leader, a wounded guard with crucial information, and a mysterious traveler offering aid. A letter found on a captured orc reveals clues to the raiders' plans.

Flexibility and Improvisation

While preparation is crucial, flexibility and improvisation are equally important. Players often make unexpected choices, and the ability to adapt the story on the fly is a valuable skill for any DM.

Techniques for Flexibility

1. **Sandbox Elements**: Design elements that players can explore in any order, giving them freedom of choice.
2. **Adapting Encounters**: Adjust encounters based on the party's actions, strengths, and weaknesses. Be ready to modify combat difficulty or the nature of social interactions.
3. **Player Input**: Encourage player input and collaboration in the story. Allow their decisions to shape the narrative and the world around them.

Example of Flexibility and Improvisation

The party decides to ignore the village leader's request and instead investigate a nearby abandoned castle they heard rumors about. The DM quickly adapts by moving some planned encounters to the castle, ensuring the session remains engaging and relevant to the overall plot.

Final Thoughts on Preparing Your Campaign

Preparing a D&D campaign is a blend of creativity, organization, and adaptability. By crafting a rich world, compelling plot, and diverse encounters, and by being prepared to adjust based on player actions, you can create a memorable and enjoyable experience for your players. Remember, the goal is to foster collaborative storytelling and fun, where both you and your players contribute to the unfolding adventure.

Creating NPCs and Monsters

Creating NPCs

Non-player characters (NPCs) are the lifeblood of a Dungeon Master's (DM) world. They populate the setting, provide quests, and interact with the player characters (PCs). Creating compelling NPCs involves more than just stats; it requires developing personalities, motivations, and roles in the story.

Developing NPC Personalities

1. **Background and Motivations**: Understand the history and desires of your NPCs. What drives them? What are their goals and fears?
2. **Personality Traits**: Define key personality traits that make each NPC unique. This could include their demeanor, speaking style, and mannerisms.
3. **Relationships**: Determine the NPC's relationships with other characters and factions. This adds depth and context to their interactions.

Example of NPC Personalities

NPC Name: Captain Thorne, the city guard captain.

Background: A veteran soldier who fought in the last great war, now dedicated to protecting his city.

Motivations: Driven by a sense of duty and a desire to keep his family safe.

Personality Traits: Stern, no-nonsense, but with a hidden soft spot for children.

Relationships: Respected by his men, distrustful of the city's politicians, and secretly indebted to a local crime lord.

Designing NPC Roles

1. **Quest Givers**: NPCs who provide the party with missions and objectives. Ensure their motivations align with the quest they are giving.
2. **Merchants and Service Providers**: NPCs who sell goods and offer services. Detail their inventory and pricing, and consider their business ethics.
3. **Allies and Rivals**: NPCs who aid or oppose the party. Allies may provide support or resources, while rivals create conflict and competition.

Example of NPC Roles

Quest Giver: Lady Morgana, a noble seeking to recover her stolen family heirloom.

Merchant: Bregor, a dwarven blacksmith with a fondness for ale and a reputation for crafting fine weapons.

Ally: Elara, a rogue who shares a common enemy with the party.

Rival: Lord Blackwood, a rival adventurer with competing interests and a personal grudge against one of the PCs.

Creating Engaging Interactions

1. **Dialogue**: Craft realistic and engaging dialogue for NPCs. Avoid clichés and strive for unique voices.
2. **Choices and Consequences**: Present the players with meaningful choices in their interactions with NPCs. Ensure their decisions have tangible consequences.
3. **Dynamic Relationships**: Allow NPC relationships to evolve based on the party's actions. An ally might become an enemy, or a rival might become a begrudging friend.

Example of Engaging Interactions

The party meets Lady Morgana, who asks them to retrieve her stolen heirloom. They can choose to accept her quest, demand higher payment, or investigate her motives. Depending on their actions, Morgana might become a trusted ally or a vengeful enemy.

Creating Monsters

Monsters are the primary adversaries the party will face. Creating memorable and challenging monsters involves more than just choosing stats from the Monster Manual.

Customizing Monsters

1. **Adjusting Stats**: Modify the hit points, attack bonuses, and abilities of existing monsters to fit the desired challenge level.
2. **Unique Abilities**: Add unique abilities or attacks to make the monster stand out. This could include special attacks, resistances, or environmental adaptations.
3. **Lore and Background**: Develop a backstory for the monster. Why is it here? What are its goals? This adds depth to the encounter.

Example of Customizing Monsters

Monster: Frost Giant

Adjusted Stats: Increased hit points to 200, added resistance to cold damage.

Unique Abilities: Can create a blizzard once per day, reducing visibility and causing cold damage over time.

Lore: The frost giant, named Grimgar, is the last of his clan, seeking revenge on those who destroyed his family.

Designing Monster Encounters

1. **Environmental Context**: Place monsters in environments that make sense and provide tactical challenges. A fire-breathing

dragon in a volcanic lair, or a band of goblins in a dense forest.
2. **Tactical Complexity**: Design encounters that require strategic thinking. Use terrain, traps, and multiple types of monsters to create dynamic battles.
3. **Narrative Integration**: Ensure the monster encounter fits within the story. Why is the monster here? How does it relate to the current quest or plot?

Example of Designing Monster Encounters

The party must navigate a frozen tundra to find an ancient artifact. They encounter Grimgar, the frost giant, in his icy fortress. The fortress is filled with treacherous ice bridges, hidden traps, and Grimgar's minions. The encounter is not just a fight, but a challenge of survival and strategy.

Running Encounters and Adventures

Structuring an Adventure

An adventure is a series of encounters and events that form a cohesive narrative. Proper structuring ensures a balanced mix of exploration, roleplaying, and combat.

Adventure Outline

1. **Introduction**: Present the adventure hook and set the stage for the players. This could be a call to action, a mysterious event, or a direct request from an NPC.
2. **Rising Action**: Build tension with a series of challenges and encounters that lead up to the climax. Include opportunities for roleplaying, exploration, and combat.
3. **Climax**: The peak of the adventure, usually involving a significant battle or critical decision. This should be the most intense and engaging part of the session.
4. **Falling Action**: Resolve the immediate aftermath of the climax. The players see the consequences of their actions and begin to wind down.
5. **Conclusion**: Wrap up the adventure. Provide rewards, tie up loose ends, and set up future adventures.

Example of an Adventure Outline

Adventure Name: The Cursed Village

Introduction: The party arrives in a village plagued by mysterious disappearances. The village elder begs for their help.

Rising Action: The party investigates the disappearances, facing challenges like hostile wildlife, suspicious villagers, and cryptic clues leading to an ancient crypt.

Climax: In the crypt, they discover the source of the curse—a vengeful spirit. They must defeat the spirit and break the curse.

Falling Action: With the spirit defeated, the village begins to recover. The party is hailed as heroes.

Conclusion: The village elder rewards the party with gold and a map hinting at their next adventure.

Running Encounters

Encounters are the building blocks of an adventure, providing moments of action, tension, and decision-making.

Types of Encounters

1. **Combat Encounters**: Involve battles with monsters or hostile NPCs. These test the party's tactical skills and resource management.
2. **Social Encounters**: Involve interaction with NPCs. These test the party's roleplaying and persuasion skills.
3. **Exploration Encounters**: Involve navigating and interacting with the

environment. These test the party's ingenuity and perception.

Example of Types of Encounters

Combat Encounter: The party is ambushed by bandits while traveling through a dense forest. They must use their combat skills to survive.

Social Encounter: The party negotiates with a local merchant for a rare item needed for their quest. Success depends on their persuasion and diplomacy.

Exploration Encounter: The party navigates a trapped tomb to find a hidden treasure. Success depends on their perception and problem-solving skills.

Balancing Encounters

1. **Challenge Rating (CR)**: Use the CR system to gauge the difficulty of combat encounters. Ensure a mix of easy, moderate, and challenging encounters.
2. **Variety**: Vary the types of encounters to keep the game dynamic. Balance combat with social and exploration challenges.
3. **Pacing**: Manage the pacing of encounters to maintain player engagement. Alternate between intense action and slower, investigative moments.

Example of Balancing Encounters

In an adventure, the DM plans:

- A moderate combat encounter with a pack of wolves (CR 1).
- A challenging social encounter with a suspicious guard captain (CR 3 equivalent).
- An easy exploration encounter involving a puzzle to open a secret door.

Running Adventures

Running adventures involves not just presenting encounters but also guiding the story, maintaining engagement, and adapting to player actions.

Maintaining Engagement

1. **Player Agency**: Give players meaningful choices that affect the story. Avoid railroading them into predetermined paths.
2. **Interactive Environments**: Design environments that players can interact with in creative ways. Encourage exploration and experimentation.
3. **Dynamic Storytelling**: Keep the story dynamic and responsive to player actions. Be ready to adapt your plans based on their decisions.

Example of Maintaining Engagement

During an investigation, the players decide to split up to cover more ground. The DM adapts by presenting different clues and challenges for each group, ensuring everyone remains engaged.

Adapting to Player Actions

1. **Improvisation**: Be prepared to improvise when players take unexpected actions. This keeps the game fluid and responsive.
2. **Flexible Plot Points**: Design plot points that can be moved or adjusted based on player actions. This ensures the story can continue smoothly.
3. **Player Feedback**: Encourage and incorporate player feedback. This helps tailor the game to their preferences and enhances their investment.

Example of Adapting to Player Actions

The party decides to ally with a previously hostile faction to achieve their goal. The DM adjusts the storyline, incorporating this alliance and its consequences into the adventure.

Building Your World

Map Creation and Worldbuilding

Creating a world for your Dungeons & Dragons (D&D) campaign is an intricate process that involves designing geography, cultures, politics, and histories. This chapter will guide you through the essential steps of map creation and worldbuilding to construct a rich and immersive setting for your players.

Map Creation

Maps are vital tools for visualizing and organizing your world. They help both you and your players understand the geography, navigate the terrain, and locate important places.

Designing Your World Map

1. **Geographical Features**: Start by outlining the major geographical features of your world, such as continents, oceans, mountains, rivers, forests, and deserts. Consider how these features interact with each other and influence the world's climate and ecosystems.
2. **Regions and Borders**: Divide your world into different regions or countries. Define their borders, natural or political, and consider how geography affects the culture and development of these regions.
3. **Key Locations**: Identify and mark important locations, including cities, towns, villages, dungeons, and landmarks. Think about their strategic importance, historical significance, and their roles in your campaign.
4. **Scale and Distance**: Decide on the scale of your map. Determine how large each region is and how long it takes to travel between key locations. This helps in planning journeys and understanding the scope of your world.

Example of World Map Design

In a high-fantasy world, you might create a continent called Eldoria. It features a central mountain range called the Spine of the World, with lush forests to the east and arid deserts to the west.

The Kingdom of Valoria lies to the north, while the Empire of Drakonia dominates the southern region. Major cities like Valoria City, Drakonspire, and the port town of Seaport are marked on the map, along with ancient ruins and hidden caves.

Creating Regional Maps

1. **Detailed Geography**: Zoom in on specific regions to create more detailed maps. Focus on the layout of cities, the arrangement of smaller geographical features, and the locations of significant landmarks.
2. **Local Features**: Include local features such as farms, mines, trade routes, and smaller settlements. These details add depth to the world and provide additional points of interest for your players.
3. **Dynamic Elements**: Consider how events in your campaign might change the regional map over time. For instance, a city could grow, a forest could burn down, or a new fortress could be constructed.

Example of Regional Map Creation

For the Kingdom of Valoria, create a detailed map showing Valoria City at the center, surrounded by smaller towns like Riverwood and Stonehaven. The map includes trade routes connecting these locations, forests with hidden bandit camps, and rivers that provide natural barriers and resources.

Utilizing Map Tools

1. **Hand-Drawn Maps**: Hand-drawing maps can add a personal touch and creativity to your world. Use graph paper or sketching tools to design your maps.
2. **Digital Tools**: Digital map-making tools, such as Campaign Cartographer, Inkarnate, or Wonderdraft, offer advanced features and professional-quality results. They allow you to create detailed, customizable maps with ease.
3. **Interactive Maps**: Consider using interactive maps that players can explore digitally. Tools like Roll20 or Foundry VTT allow you to upload maps and create interactive elements for online play.

Example of Using Digital Tools

Using Inkarnate, create a detailed map of Eldoria with lush forests, detailed cityscapes, and dynamic weather effects. Share the map with your players via Roll20, allowing them to interact with the world and explore key locations during sessions.

Worldbuilding

Worldbuilding involves creating the cultures, politics, histories, and mythologies that breathe life into your world. This process transforms your map into a living, dynamic setting.

Creating Cultures and Societies

1. **Races and Ethnicities**: Define the races and ethnicities that inhabit your world. Consider their physical traits, cultural practices, and societal norms. How do they interact with each other?
2. **Languages and Dialects**: Determine the languages spoken in your world. Consider regional dialects and how language influences culture and communication.
3. **Customs and Traditions**: Develop customs, traditions, and holidays unique to each culture. These elements add depth and richness to the world, providing players with immersive experiences.

Example of Cultural Worldbuilding

In Eldoria, the Kingdom of Valoria is primarily inhabited by humans, known for their valor and chivalry. They celebrate the annual Festival of Lights, a tradition marking the end of winter and the return of longer days. The neighboring elven forest, Elarion, is home to the reclusive Elarian elves, who speak an ancient dialect and practice elaborate rituals to honor their forest spirits.

Establishing Politics and Power Dynamics

1. **Governments and Rulers**: Define the political systems and structures of power in your world. Who rules each region, and how do they maintain control? Consider monarchies, democracies, theocracies, and other forms of governance.
2. **Political Relationships**: Map out the relationships between different regions and factions. Are they allies, rivals, or neutral? What treaties, conflicts, or alliances shape these dynamics?
3. **Factions and Organizations**: Create influential factions and organizations that operate within your world. These could include guilds, secret societies, religious orders, and mercenary groups. Define their goals, resources, and influence.

Example of Political Worldbuilding

In Eldoria, the Kingdom of Valoria is ruled by King Alaric, a just and wise monarch. The Empire of Drakonia, to the south, is governed by Empress Seraphina, who seeks to expand her territory. The two nations are in a tenuous truce, but tensions remain high. The Thieves' Guild operates in the shadows, manipulating events for their own gain, while the Order of the Silver Flame, a religious order, seeks to protect the realm from dark forces.

Developing Histories and Mythologies

1. **Historical Events**: Outline significant historical events that have shaped your world. These could include wars, natural disasters, political upheavals, and cultural renaissances. Consider how these events influence the present day.
2. **Mythology and Religion**: Create the myths, legends, and religious beliefs of your world. Define the pantheon of gods, creation myths, and religious practices. How do these beliefs shape the culture and actions of your inhabitants?
3. **Legends and Folklore**: Develop local legends and folklore that add flavor to your world. These stories can inspire adventures and provide hooks for your players.

Example of Historical and Mythological Worldbuilding

Eldoria's history is marked by the War of the Shattered Crown, a devastating conflict between Valoria and Drakonia that ended in a fragile peace. The world was created by the gods during the Age of Dawn, according to the ancient texts of the Church of the Silver Flame. Local legends tell of the Lost City of Zarlath, a mythical city said to hold untold treasures and guarded by ancient spirits.

Lore and Storytelling

Lore and storytelling are essential for immersing players in your world. Crafting detailed lore and integrating it into your narrative can make your world feel alive and compelling.

Crafting Compelling Lore

1. **Consistency and Depth**: Ensure your lore is consistent and deep. Avoid contradictions and build a coherent history and mythology. Detail the origins of major cities, the rise and fall of empires, and the evolution of cultures.
2. **Interconnected Stories**: Weave interconnected stories that span different regions and time periods. Show how events in one part of the world influence another.
3. **Player Involvement**: Incorporate players' backstories into your world's lore. This makes the world feel personal and gives players a sense of ownership over the story.

Example of Crafting Lore

Eldoria's lore includes the tale of the Dragon Wars, a series of conflicts where dragons ruled the skies and terrorized the land. Heroes of old, armed with magical weapons forged by the gods, defeated the dragons and established the modern kingdoms. The legacy of these heroes is felt in the present, with their descendants holding positions of power and their artifacts sought after by adventurers.

Integrating Lore into Gameplay

1. **Exposition Through Exploration**: Reveal lore through exploration and discovery. Ancient ruins, forgotten libraries, and hidden artifacts can provide players with insights into the world's history.
2. **Dialogue and Interaction**: Use NPCs to share lore through dialogue and interactions. Wise sages, wandering bards, and local historians can provide players with knowledge and context.
3. **Quests and Adventures**: Design quests and adventures that are rooted in the world's lore. This makes the story feel organic and integrated with the setting.

Example of Integrating Lore

As the party explores the ancient ruins of Zarlath, they find murals depicting the Dragon Wars and uncover a hidden library with scrolls detailing the fall of the dragonlords. A local historian, seeking to restore the lost knowledge, becomes an invaluable ally, guiding the party to key locations and providing historical context.

Final Thoughts on Building Your World

Building a world for your D&D campaign is a creative and rewarding process. By designing detailed maps, crafting rich cultures and histories, and integrating compelling lore into your narrative, you create an immersive and engaging setting for your players. Remember to be flexible and responsive to player actions, allowing your world to evolve and grow organically. The ultimate goal is to create a living, dynamic world where epic adventures and unforgettable stories unfold.

Designing Dungeons and Cities

Creating compelling dungeons and vibrant cities is an essential part of worldbuilding in Dungeons & Dragons (D&D). This chapter will guide you through the intricacies of designing dungeons and cities, ensuring they are engaging, dynamic, and integral to your campaign.

Designing Dungeons

Dungeons are a staple of D&D, offering opportunities for exploration, combat, and problem-solving. A well-designed dungeon can provide memorable challenges and a sense of accomplishment for your players.

Conceptualizing Your Dungeon

1. **Theme and Purpose**: Determine the theme and purpose of your dungeon. Is it an ancient tomb, a wizard's tower, a bandit hideout, or a natural cave? Understanding its purpose helps guide the design and the type of challenges it will present.
2. **Lore and Backstory**: Develop the backstory of the dungeon. Who built it? Why does it exist? What events have transpired within its walls? This lore adds depth and context to the dungeon, making it more than just a series of rooms and corridors.
3. **Environment and Atmosphere**: Consider the environment and atmosphere of the dungeon. Is it dark and foreboding, filled with traps and undead? Or is it a mystical place, brimming with magical energies and ancient secrets? Use descriptions to evoke a vivid sense of place.

Example of Conceptualizing a Dungeon

Imagine an ancient dwarven stronghold, long abandoned and now infested with goblins. The stronghold, known as Khazad-Dûm, was built to protect a powerful artifact, the Heart of the Mountain. Over centuries, the stronghold fell to goblins, and now the players must navigate its dark, trap-laden halls to retrieve the artifact.

Designing the Layout

1. **Map Design**: Create a map of your dungeon. Sketch out rooms, corridors, and key locations. Ensure there is a logical flow, but include branches and dead ends to encourage exploration and make the dungeon feel expansive.
2. **Room Types**: Design a variety of rooms to keep the dungeon interesting. Include combat arenas, puzzle rooms, traps, treasure chambers, and rest areas. Each room should serve a specific purpose and contribute to the overall theme.
3. **Verticality and Complexity**: Add vertical elements such as staircases, ladders, and pits to make the dungeon more complex. Multi-level dungeons provide additional challenges and opportunities for creative problem-solving.

Example of Dungeon Layout

In Khazad-Dûm, the entrance leads to a grand hall with broken statues of dwarven kings. From there, players can explore side chambers filled with goblin camps, a deep pit leading to the lower mines, and a treasure room guarded by a powerful goblin shaman. Secret passages and hidden doors offer shortcuts and alternative routes.

Populating the Dungeon

1. **Monsters and NPCs**: Populate your dungeon with appropriate monsters and NPCs. Consider the dungeon's history and environment when choosing inhabitants. Goblins, undead, and constructs are common, but unique creatures add flavor.
2. **Traps and Hazards**: Incorporate traps and hazards to challenge players. Pitfalls, poison darts, collapsing ceilings, and magical wards are just a few examples. Ensure traps are fair and provide clues for cautious players to detect and disarm them.
3. **Treasure and Rewards**: Place treasure and rewards strategically. Include valuable items, gold, magical artifacts, and lore pieces that tie into the dungeon's backstory. Ensure rewards are balanced with the dungeon's difficulty.

Example of Populating a Dungeon

Khazad-Dûm is filled with goblin patrols, giant spiders in the lower mines, and animated stone guardians near the artifact chamber. Traps include collapsing bridges over chasms and poison gas in treasure rooms. Rewards include dwarven gold, enchanted weapons, and the Heart of the Mountain, a powerful magical gem.

Designing Cities

Cities serve as hubs of civilization and adventure in D&D. A well-designed city provides a rich tapestry of social interactions, quests, and resources.

Conceptualizing Your City

1. **City Theme and History**: Define the theme and history of your city. Is it a bustling trade hub, a mystical elven enclave, or a fortified military outpost? Develop its historical background, founding events, and significant changes over time.
2. **Districts and Layout**: Divide the city into distinct districts, each with its own character and purpose. Common districts include residential areas, marketplaces, noble quarters, slums, and entertainment zones. Design the layout to facilitate ease of navigation and exploration.
3. **Key Landmarks**: Identify key landmarks that define the city's identity. These could be castles, temples, guild halls, markets, statues, or unique natural features. Landmarks provide focal points for storytelling and navigation.

Example of Conceptualizing a City

Valoria City is the capital of the Kingdom of Valoria, known for its grand architecture and rich history. Founded by King Valorian the Great, it has grown into a major trade and cultural center. Districts include the Royal Quarter, the Merchant's Ward, the Slums of Darkwater, and the Temple District. Key landmarks are the Royal Palace, the Grand Market, and the Cathedral of the Silver Flame.

Designing the Layout

1. **Map Design**: Create a map of your city, marking districts, streets, and landmarks. Ensure the layout makes sense for the city's size and function. Consider natural barriers like rivers and hills.
2. **Buildings and Interiors**: Detail important buildings and their interiors. Include taverns, shops, temples, homes, and other locations where players can interact with NPCs and find quests.
3. **Street Life and Atmosphere**: Describe the city's atmosphere. Is it bustling with activity, or quiet and eerie? Populate the streets with vendors, guards, beggars, and entertainers. This brings the city to life and provides players with immersive experiences.

Example of City Layout

Valoria City's map shows the Royal Quarter in the center, surrounded by the Merchant's Ward to the north, the Temple District to the east, and the Slums of Darkwater to the south. The Grand Market is a bustling hub in the Merchant's Ward, while the Cathedral of the Silver Flame dominates the Temple District. Streets are filled with merchants hawking goods, guards patrolling, and citizens going about their daily lives.

Populating the City

1. **NPCs and Factions**: Populate the city with diverse NPCs and factions. Include merchants, guards, nobles, thieves, priests, and adventurers. Develop their personalities, motivations, and relationships with each other.
2. **Quests and Interactions**: Design quests and interactions that players can find in the city. These could range from simple fetch quests to complex political intrigues. Ensure quests are tied to the city's history and factions.
3. **Dynamic Elements**: Introduce dynamic elements such as events, festivals, or crises that affect the city. These elements create a sense of a living, changing world.

Example of Populating a City

Valoria City is home to NPCs like Marcus the Merchant, who deals in rare goods; Captain Elena, the head of the city guard; and Brother Alden, a priest at the Cathedral of the Silver Flame. Factions include the Merchant's Guild, the Thieves' Guild, and the Order of the Silver Flame. Quests range from helping Marcus recover stolen goods to assisting Captain Elena in uncovering a plot against the king.

Crafting Side Quests

Side quests are essential for enriching your campaign, offering players opportunities to explore the world, develop their characters, and gain rewards outside the main storyline.

Types of Side Quests

1. **Fetch Quests**: Simple quests where players retrieve items for NPCs. These can be used to introduce players to new locations and NPCs.
2. **Escort Quests**: Quests where players protect NPCs as they travel to a destination. These often involve combat and strategic planning.
3. **Investigation Quests**: Quests that require players to solve mysteries or uncover secrets. These involve gathering clues, interviewing NPCs, and piecing together information.

4. **Combat Quests**: Quests focused on defeating specific enemies or clearing out areas of monsters. These provide opportunities for tactical combat and gaining combat experience.
5. **Crafting and Trade Quests**: Quests that involve creating items or engaging in trade. These can highlight players' crafting skills and economic acumen.
6. **Character-Driven Quests**: Quests that are personal to the characters, involving their backgrounds, goals, or relationships. These quests deepen character development and player engagement.

Designing Side Quests

1. **Hook and Motivation**: Create a compelling hook to draw players into the side quest. Ensure the quest provides clear motivation, whether it's for reward, altruism, or personal interest.
2. **Objectives and Challenges**: Define clear objectives and challenges. These could include finding specific items, defeating enemies, solving puzzles, or making moral decisions.
3. **Integration with Main Story**: Integrate side quests with the main story. They should feel like natural extensions of the world and

provide additional context or background to the primary narrative.

Example of Crafting a Side Quest

In Valoria City, the players encounter Marcus the Merchant, who asks them to retrieve a rare herb from the dangerous Darkwood Forest for a special potion. The quest involves navigating the forest, dealing with its wildlife, and uncovering a hidden bandit camp. Success earns the players Marcus's gratitude, a discount at his shop, and an introduction to other influential merchants.

Balancing Rewards and Risks

1. **Appropriate Rewards**: Ensure rewards are appropriate for the quest's difficulty and the players' level. Rewards could include gold, magical items, experience points, or new allies.
2. **Scaling Challenges**: Scale the challenges to match the players' abilities. Ensure combat encounters, puzzles, and other challenges are neither too easy nor too difficult.
3. **Meaningful Consequences**: Design quests with meaningful consequences. Players' choices and actions should have lasting effects on the world and NPCs, adding weight to their decisions.

Example of Balancing Rewards and Risks

For the Darkwood Forest quest, players face challenging combat with bandits and wild beasts. The reward, a potent healing potion and a valuable herb, matches the difficulty. Additionally, their actions influence the bandits' future activities, potentially leading to further quests or consequences.

Integrating Side Quests into the World

1. **Location-Specific Quests**: Design side quests that are specific to locations within your world. These quests should leverage the unique features and history of the locations.
2. **NPC Relationships**: Use side quests to develop relationships with NPCs. Completing quests can earn players allies, resources, and information that impact future adventures.
3. **World Events**: Incorporate world events that generate side quests. Festivals, disasters, political changes, and other events can provide new quest opportunities.

Example of Integrating Side Quests

In Valoria City, side quests include helping Brother Alden at the Cathedral of the Silver Flame to find a stolen relic, or assisting Captain Elena with a jailbreak in the Slums of Darkwater. These quests utilize the city's unique districts and NPCs, enriching the players' experience and deepening their connection to the world.

Advanced Gameplay

Multiclassing and Feats

Multiclassing

Multiclassing allows a character to gain levels in multiple classes, combining the strengths and abilities of each. This can create versatile and unique characters but requires careful planning to balance the character's abilities and maintain effectiveness in gameplay.

Understanding Multiclassing

1. **Basic Concept**: Multiclassing involves taking levels in a new class instead of continuing to advance in the character's original class. For example, a 5th-level Fighter might take their next level as a Wizard, becoming a Fighter 5/Wizard 1.
2. **Requirements**: To multiclass, a character must meet certain ability score prerequisites. These prerequisites ensure that the character has the necessary skills and traits to learn and perform the new class's abilities.

- **Fighter**: Requires Strength 13 or Dexterity 13.
- **Wizard**: Requires Intelligence 13.
- Other classes have similar requirements, detailed in the Player's Handbook.

3. **Class Features and Abilities**: When a character multiclasses, they gain the new class's features but must track their progression separately for each class. This affects hit points, proficiencies, spellcasting, and other abilities.

Example of Multiclassing

Consider a 6th-level Rogue who wants to multiclass into a Fighter. The Rogue must have at least 13 in Strength or Dexterity. Upon taking the first level in Fighter, the character gains proficiency with medium armor, shields, and martial weapons, the Fighting Style feature, and Second Wind, while retaining all Rogue abilities up to 6th level.

Benefits and Drawbacks

1. **Benefits**:
   - **Versatility**: Multiclassing allows characters to gain a broader range of abilities, making them more versatile in various situations.
   - **Customization**: Players can create unique combinations that fit their character concepts and playstyles.
2. **Drawbacks**:

- **Delayed Progression**: Multiclassing can delay access to higher-level abilities and features of a single class.
- **Complexity**: Managing multiple class features and abilities can be more complex and challenging.

Example of Benefits and Drawbacks

A Wizard who multiclasses into Cleric gains access to healing spells and divine abilities but delays their progression to higher-level wizard spells. This trade-off can be advantageous in a party needing support but requires careful management of spell slots and abilities.

Popular Multiclass Combinations

1. **Fighter/Rogue**: Combines combat prowess with stealth and cunning. The Fighter's durability and combat abilities complement the Rogue's sneak attack and skills.
2. **Cleric/Paladin**: Blends divine magic and martial abilities. The Cleric's healing and support spells enhance the Paladin's combat effectiveness and smiting abilities.
3. **Wizard/Sorcerer**: Merges arcane knowledge with innate magical abilities. This combination allows for a wide range of spellcasting options and versatility in magical combat.

Example of Popular Combination

A Fighter 3/Rogue 3 character can utilize the Fighter's Action Surge to attack multiple times in one turn, then use the Rogue's Cunning Action to disengage or hide. This creates a highly mobile and deadly combatant.

Feats

Feats are special abilities that provide characters with unique capabilities and enhancements. They offer a way to customize and specialize characters beyond their class features and ability score improvements.

Understanding Feats

1. **Basic Concept**: Feats are optional and can be chosen instead of increasing ability scores when a character reaches certain levels. Each feat provides specific benefits that enhance or add new abilities.
2. **Choosing Feats**: When selecting a feat, consider the character's class, role in the party, and playstyle. Some feats are more beneficial for certain classes or character concepts.
3. **Types of Feats**: Feats can enhance combat abilities, skills, spellcasting, or provide new proficiencies. They vary widely in their effects and applications.

Example of Feats

- **Sharpshooter**: Allows a character to take a penalty to hit with ranged attacks in exchange for increased damage. Ideal for ranged combatants like Rangers or Archers.
- **Resilient**: Increases one ability score by 1 and grants proficiency in saving throws for that

ability. Useful for characters needing to shore up weaknesses.
- **War Caster**: Grants advantages on concentration checks, the ability to cast spells while holding weapons or shields, and the ability to cast a spell as a reaction to an opportunity attack. Perfect for spellcasters in melee combat.

Popular Feats

1. **Great Weapon Master**: Provides benefits for characters using heavy weapons, allowing them to make additional attacks or deal extra damage. Ideal for Barbarians and Fighters.
2. **Lucky**: Grants a number of rerolls for attacks, ability checks, or saving throws. This versatile feat is beneficial for any class.
3. **Mobile**: Increases movement speed and allows a character to avoid opportunity attacks after making a melee attack. Perfect for melee characters who need to move quickly in and out of combat.

Example of Popular Feat

A Fighter with the Great Weapon Master feat can take a -5 penalty to attack rolls in exchange for +10 to damage. Combined with the Fighter's Action Surge, this can result in devastating damage output in a single round.

Homebrewing Rules and Content

Homebrewing involves creating custom rules, content, and modifications to the game. This allows Dungeon Masters (DMs) and players to tailor their games to fit their preferences and enhance the storytelling experience.

Understanding Homebrewing

1. **Basic Concept**: Homebrewing is the process of creating custom content that is not part of the official D&D rules. This can include new races, classes, spells, items, and rules.
2. **Purpose**: Homebrewing allows DMs to personalize their campaigns, address specific player needs, and introduce unique elements that enhance the game.

Homebrewing New Races

1. **Concept and Theme**: Start with a clear concept and theme for the new race. Consider their culture, appearance, abilities, and lore.
2. **Ability Scores and Traits**: Define the race's ability score increases and racial traits. Balance these traits against existing races to ensure fairness.
3. **Playtesting and Feedback**: Test the new race with your players and gather feedback. Adjust traits and abilities as needed to maintain balance and fun.

Example of Homebrewing a Race

The Aarakocra, a bird-like race with the ability to fly, can be homebrewed by adjusting their traits for a specific campaign. If flight is too powerful, consider limiting it to certain levels or creating environmental challenges that restrict flying.

Homebrewing New Classes and Subclasses

1. **Concept and Role**: Define the new class or subclass's role in the party and its unique features. Ensure it fills a niche not covered by existing classes.
2. **Abilities and Progression**: Design the class's abilities and how they progress with levels. Balance these against other classes to ensure they are neither too powerful nor too weak.
3. **Playtesting and Iteration**: Test the new class in various scenarios. Gather player feedback and iterate on the design to refine balance and functionality.

Example of Homebrewing a Class

Creating a Witch class might involve combining elements of spellcasting and nature magic. Design unique abilities like Hexes or Curses that differentiate it from Wizards and Druids. Ensure balance by comparing spell progression and abilities with existing classes.

Homebrewing New Spells and Magic Items

1. **Spell Design**: Define the spell's level, components, range, duration, and effects. Ensure

it aligns with the power level of other spells at the same level.
2. **Item Creation**: Design magic items with unique abilities. Balance their power with existing magic items and consider their rarity and cost.
3. **Testing and Adjustment**: Test new spells and items in gameplay. Adjust their effects and balance based on player feedback and game impact.

Example of Homebrewing a Spell

Creating a spell like "Storm's Fury" might involve defining it as a 5th-level evocation spell that calls down a lightning storm. Specify damage, area of effect, and additional effects like knocking enemies prone. Compare it with existing 5th-level spells to ensure balance.

Balancing Homebrew Content

1. **Consistency with Core Rules**: Ensure homebrew content is consistent with the core rules and mechanics of D&D. This helps maintain coherence and ease of integration.
2. **Fairness and Fun**: Balance homebrew content to be fair and fun for all players. Avoid creating content that overshadows or diminishes other players' abilities.
3. **Flexibility and Adaptation**: Be willing to adapt and adjust homebrew content based on gameplay experiences. Flexibility ensures that

homebrew content enhances rather than disrupts the game.

Example of Balancing Homebrew Content

If a homebrewed magic item proves too powerful, adjust its abilities or impose limitations. For instance, a sword that grants extra attacks might be balanced by requiring attunement and limiting its use to specific circumstances.

Integrating Homebrew Content into Your Campaign

1. **Story Integration**: Seamlessly integrate homebrew content into your campaign's story and setting. Provide lore and context that make the content feel natural and coherent.
2. **Player Involvement**: Involve players in the homebrewing process. Solicit their ideas and feedback to create content that resonates with the group.
3. **Documentation and Clarity**: Document homebrew rules and content clearly. Ensure all players understand and agree to the new elements to avoid confusion and disputes.

Example of Integrating Homebrew Content

Introduce a homebrewed artifact, the "Crystal of Eldara," with a rich backstory tied to the campaign's main plot. Involve players in quests to discover its origins and unlock its powers, making it an integral part of their adventure.

Complex Combat Tactics

Understanding Complex Combat Tactics

Combat in Dungeons & Dragons can range from simple skirmishes to highly strategic battles involving intricate maneuvers and tactics. Mastering complex combat tactics can make encounters more engaging and challenging, enhancing the overall gameplay experience.

Tactical Positioning

1. **Flanking**: Positioning characters on opposite sides of an enemy to gain advantage on attack rolls. This requires coordination and teamwork but can significantly increase the chances of hitting the target.
2. **Choke Points**: Utilizing narrow spaces or terrain features to limit enemy movement and focus attacks. This is especially useful when facing a numerically superior force.
3. **Cover and Concealment**: Using environmental features like walls, trees, or magical barriers to gain cover, which provides a bonus to AC and Dexterity saving throws. Concealment can also obscure vision, making it harder for enemies to hit or target characters.

Example of Tactical Positioning

In a dungeon corridor, the party encounters a group of orcs. The Fighter and Paladin move to block the narrow passage, creating a choke point. Meanwhile, the Rogue and Ranger position themselves behind the orcs to gain flanking advantages, while the Wizard stays back behind cover to cast spells without being targeted.

Coordinated Attacks

1. **Focus Fire**: Concentrating attacks on a single enemy to quickly reduce their numbers. This tactic is effective for eliminating high-priority targets like spellcasters or leaders.
2. **Setting Traps**: Using spells, abilities, or items to set traps or ambushes. This can involve laying caltrops, casting spells like *Grease* or *Web*, or using illusions to mislead enemies.
3. **Combining Abilities**: Coordinating abilities and spells to create powerful combinations. For example, a Druid's *Entangle* spell followed by a Wizard's *Fireball* can trap and damage multiple enemies simultaneously.

Example of Coordinated Attacks

The party encounters a powerful necromancer and his undead minions. The Rogue uses *Stealth* to get into position and then delivers a *Sneak Attack* to the necromancer. The Cleric follows up with *Turn Undead*, causing the minions to flee, while the Fighter and Barbarian focus their attacks on the weakened necromancer.

Defensive Tactics

1. **Retreat and Regroup**: Knowing when to retreat and regroup can save the party from total defeat. Strategic retreats can lead to better positioning or recovery opportunities.
2. **Defensive Formations**: Forming defensive lines or circles to protect weaker members of the party, such as spellcasters or wounded allies.
3. **Using Defensive Spells**: Spells like *Shield*, *Sanctuary*, or *Counterspell* can protect the party from harm or disrupt enemy plans.

Example of Defensive Tactics

During a tough battle against a dragon, the party realizes they are outmatched. The Paladin uses *Lay on Hands* to heal the Wizard, who then casts *Wall of Force* to create a temporary barrier. The party retreats to a defensible position to regroup and plan their next move.

High-Level Play

High-level play in Dungeons & Dragons introduces new challenges, opportunities, and complexities. Characters at higher levels possess powerful abilities and spells that can shape the course of entire campaigns. Understanding the nuances of high-level play is crucial for both players and Dungeon Masters.

High-Level Abilities and Spells

1. **Powerful Spells**: High-level spellcasters gain access to spells of 6th level and above, which can have dramatic effects on the game. Spells like

Wish, *Meteor Swarm*, and *Time Stop* can alter reality, deal massive damage, or manipulate time.
2. **Legendary Actions and Lair Actions**: High-level monsters, such as ancient dragons or powerful demons, often have legendary actions and lair actions. These abilities allow them to act outside of their normal turn order, creating dynamic and dangerous encounters.
3. **Epic Boons**: Characters who reach level 20 can gain epic boons, which are powerful enhancements that provide unique benefits. These boons can further customize and enhance characters, making them even more formidable.

Example of High-Level Abilities and Spells

A 17th-level Wizard prepares for a final confrontation with an ancient red dragon. The Wizard casts *Wish* to replicate the effects of *Mass Heal*, restoring the entire party to full health. During the battle, the dragon uses its legendary actions to attack multiple times per round, creating a challenging and dynamic encounter.

Advanced Strategic Considerations

1. **Resource Management**: High-level characters must carefully manage their resources, including spell slots, hit points, and magical items. Efficient use of resources can make the difference between victory and defeat.
2. **Political and Social Dynamics**: At higher levels, characters often become influential

figures in their world. Navigating political intrigue, forming alliances, and managing followers can become significant aspects of the game.
3. **Epic Quests and Challenges**: High-level campaigns often involve epic quests that can have world-altering consequences. These quests can include battling gods, saving entire realms, or uncovering ancient secrets.

Example of Advanced Strategic Considerations

The party, now renowned heroes, is tasked with preventing a demonic invasion. They must gather allies from various factions, manage their kingdom's resources, and undertake dangerous missions to weaken the demonic forces. Balancing these tasks requires careful planning and diplomacy.

Managing High-Level Campaigns

1. **Balancing Encounters**: High-level characters can deal and withstand significant amounts of damage. Designing balanced encounters that challenge but do not overwhelm them is crucial. This may involve using multiple powerful enemies, environmental hazards, and strategic objectives.
2. **Maintaining Player Engagement**: High-level play can sometimes lead to power imbalances. Ensuring all players remain engaged and challenged requires thoughtful encounter design and opportunities for each character to shine.

3. **Scaling Challenges**: Continuously scaling challenges to match the party's power level ensures the game remains exciting. This can include introducing new types of enemies, complex puzzles, and moral dilemmas.

Example of Managing High-Level Campaigns

The party is tasked with infiltrating an infernal citadel to retrieve an artifact that can stop the demonic invasion. The DM designs the citadel with multiple layers of defenses, including traps, powerful guardians, and a series of puzzles that require the party to work together. Each character has opportunities to use their unique abilities, ensuring a balanced and engaging experience.

Made in the USA
Columbia, SC
20 January 2025